M000035451

PRE-EMPLOYMENT SCREENING FOR PSYCHOPATHOLOGY:
A GUIDE TO PROFESSIONAL PRACTICE

Rodney L. Lowman, PhD
Divisions of Occupational Medicine
and Medical Psychology
Duke University Medical Center

Professional Resource Exchange, Inc.
Sarasota, Florida

Paperback Edition ISBN: 0-943158-34-6
Library of Congress Catalog Number: 88-43546

The copy editor for this book was Janet Sailian, the production supervisor was Debbie Fink, the graphics coordinator was Judy Warinner, and the cover designer was Bill Tabler.

ACKNOWLEDGEMENTS

Portions of this book were presented as a paper at the annual meeting of the American Nuclear Society, Dallas, Texas, June 10, 1987. That paper received the "Best Paper Award" for the Human Factors Division.

The author would like to acknowledge and thank the following for providing helpful information and/or articles: Philip Berghausen, PhD; John Berner, PhD; Laurie Eyde, PhD; and Patrick Lavin, PhD.

This guide was completed while the author was employed by Duke University Medical Center, Divisions of Occupational Medicine and Medical Psychology. Support of the project by the Division of Occupational Medicine is acknowledged.

PRACTITIONER'S RESOURCE SERIES

SERIES EDITOR

Harold H. Smith, Jr., PhD
Smith, Sikorski-Smith, PA
Largo, Florida

CONSULTING EDITORS

William D. Anton, PhD
Director, Counseling and Wellness
University of South Florida
Tampa, Florida

Judith V. Becker, PhD
Professor of Clinical Psychology
Columbia University *and*
Director of Sexual Behavior Clinic
New York State Psychiatric Institute
New York, New York

Philip C. Boswell, PhD
Independent Practice in Clinical Psychology
Coral Gables, Florida

Florence Kaslow, PhD
Director, Florida Couples and Family Institute
West Palm Beach, Florida

Peter A. Keller, PhD
Chair, Department of Psychology
Mansfield University
Mansfield, Pennsylvania

Antonio E. Puente, PhD
Associate Professor of Psychology
University of North Carolina at Wilmington
Wilmington, North Carolina

R. John Wakeman, PhD
Head, Department of Clinical Psychology
Ochsner Clinic and Ochsner Foundation Hospital
New Orleans, Louisiana

SERIES PREFACE

As a publisher of books, cassettes, and continuing education programs, the Professional Resource Exchange strives to provide mental health professionals with highly applied resources that can be used to enhance clinical skills and expand practical knowledge.

All of the titles in the *Practitioner's Resource Series* are designed to provide important new information on topics of vital concern to psychologists, clinical social workers, marriage and family therapists, psychiatrists, and other mental health professionals.

Although the focus and content of each book in this series will be quite different, there will be notable similarities:

1. Each title in the series will address a timely topic of critical clinical importance.
2. The target audience for each title will be practicing mental health professionals. Our authors were chosen for their ability to provide concrete "how-to-do-it" guidance to colleagues who are trying to increase their competence in dealing with complex clinical problems.
3. The information provided in these books will represent "state-of-the-art" information and techniques derived from both clinical experience and empirical research. Each of these guide books will include references and resources for those who wish to pursue more advanced study of the discussed topic.

4. The authors will provide numerous case studies, specific recommendations for practice, and the types of "nitty-gritty" details that clinicians need before they can incorporate new concepts and procedures into their practices.

We feel that one of the unique assets of the Professional Resource Exchange is that all of its editorial decisions are made by mental health professionals. The publisher, Larry Ritt, is a clinical psychologist and marriage and family therapist who maintains an active independent practice. The senior editor, Peter Keller, is a clinical psychologist who currently serves as chair of a psychology department and is actively involved in clinical training.

The editor of this series, Hal Smith, is a clinical psychologist in independent practice. He holds a diplomate in clinical psychology from the American Board of Professional Psychology, a diplomate in forensic psychology from the American Board of Forensic Psychology, and a diplomate in clinical neuropsychology from the American Board of Professional Neuropsychology. His specialties include clinical and forensic psychology, neuropsychology, stress management, management of chronic pain and psychophysiologic disorders, learning disabilities, interventions for spouse abusers, psychotherapy, psychodiagnostic evaluations, clinical hypnosis, and consultation.

We are also fortunate to have the services of an exceptionally well-qualified panel of consulting editors who assist in the selection and preparation of titles for this series: William D. Anton, Judith V. Becker, Philip C. Boswell, Florence Kaslow, Antonio E. Puente, and R. John Wakeman. Our consulting editors are all highly experienced clinicians. In addition, they have all made significant contributions to their professions as scholars, teachers, workshop leaders, researchers, and/or as authors and editors.

Lawrence G. Ritt, Publisher
Harold H. Smith, Jr., Series Editor

A CAUTIONARY NOTE

This book is intended to provide accurate and authoritative information about its subject. It is sold with the understanding that the publisher and the author are not engaged in rendering legal, consulting, or other professional services. If legal advice or other expert assistance is required, the services of a competent professional, with knowledge of all laws pertaining to the reader, should be sought.

ABSTRACT

This book was written to assist practitioners in conducting pre-employment screening for psychopathology in a manner that is both technically and ethically appropriate. Approaches used in this area to date vary considerably, and many significant issues of validity have gone unaddressed. Important studies in this area are reviewed, demonstrating that there is much research work still needed before definitive conclusions can be drawn about appropriate professional practice. Until this research is completed, practitioners must proceed with some caution. Traditional screening devices, such as the Minnesota Multiphasic Personality Inventory and the California Psychological Inventory, cannot be employed for purposes of pre-employment screening without modification of the usual interpretive procedures. There remain many problems with both false positives and false negatives. Specific recommendations are made for practitioners to help assure that their practices in this area are ethically and legally defensible, and for researchers who aim to provide studies that will guide future practice.

TABLE OF CONTENTS

SUMMARY OF PROFESSIONAL
PRACTICE RECOMMENDATIONS (*Continued*)

PRE-EMPLOYMENT SCREENING FOR PSYCHOPATHOLOGY: A GUIDE TO PROFESSIONAL PRACTICE

INTRODUCTION

This book is directed to psychologists and other mental health professionals who conduct pre-employment screening for psychopathology, or who are planning such activities. Intended as a guide for professional practice, this book addresses theoretical, ethical, and pragmatic issues. A major thesis is that the practice of pre-employment screening for mental impairment which may be disruptive to performance on the job has greatly surpassed underlying research findings, and that clinicians should proceed with caution when working in this area. While practitioners have important contributions to make in furthering the knowledge base for such work, clinicians must also avoid many potential pitfalls when conducting pre-employment screening, not the least of which are professional malpractice and ethical concerns.

If the clinician's primary motivation for undertaking pre-employment screening of potential employees is to diversify a practice and perhaps earn extra money, the clinician may find the legal and ethical issues to be more trouble than the revenues generated are worth. On the other hand, there are many interesting, substantive questions yet to be answered concerning appropriate professional practice in this domain, and competent clinical practice has an important potential contribution to make. The topic relates to some extremely important and relatively unexamined questions: To what extent are persons manifesting psychopathology inappropriate for

1

employment? What are the work limitations, if any, of persons with mental dysfunctions? How can the workplace enhance mental problems or make them worse? Among those showing no risk of impairment at the time of initial assessment, what is the likelihood that later psychological difficulties may impede job performance? As a practical matter, and perhaps of greatest importance, have sufficient studies been published to make possible appropriate (i.e., valid and reliable) decisions about the ability to work when psychopathology has been detected?

HISTORICAL NOTES

Pre-employment mental health screening is not a new activity. Perhaps the most widespread usage occurred (and still takes place) in the military. Estimates vary, but it has been reported that during World War II one to almost two million would-be military recruits were turned away due to mental disturbance, and that from 500,000 to a million more were discharged from active duty for mental disturbance or mental deficiency (Caveny, 1955; Glass et al., 1956). Glass et al. (1956) report that 7.2% of military selectees were rejected for neuropsychiatric reasons in the years 1942-1945, and another 4.3% were rejected during this period for reasons of mental deficiency (11.5% for the two groups combined). Comparable figures for the 1950-1953 period were 13.4% for neuropsychiatric reasons and 2.1% for mental deficiency. Clearly, however, the military practice of grouping together rejections or discharges for mental deficiency and for psychological dysfunction obscures important differences between the two groups.

Other researchers have also reported on the base rate for rejection from service for psychiatric reasons. In their follow-up study of 500 Caucasian inductees, Brill and Beebe (1952) found that about 20% had manifested psychiatric problems at the time of entry into the military. They reported that 2.2% of a group of soldiers not manifesting psychiatric disturbance at the time of induction were hospitalized for neuropsychiatric reasons during their military service, compared with a 29% hospitalization rate among those who were rated psychiatrically "marginal" at the time of induction. The latter figure rose to 35% if nonhospitalized soldiers who were administratively discharged for psychiatric reasons were also included. Aita (1949) reported that 2.5% of military

2

inductees from Ft. Snelling, Minnesota were rejected for neuropsychiatric reasons and another 5.7% were considered borderline or questionable. However, in following up a cohort of inductees, 4.7% of those in whom no psychiatric disorder was found at enlistment were reported to fail in military service, compared with 20.8% failures for those who were predicted not to be successful for psychiatric reasons. Brill and Beebe (1952) noted that about 8% of the 80% in their sample who had manifested no problems at intake were at least moderately psychiatrically disabled at the time of a 5-year follow-up. This figure was considerably lower than the groups that manifested psychopathology at time of induction.

W. A. Hunt and his associates (W. A. Hunt, Wittson, & Burton, 1950a, 1950b; W. A. Hunt, Wittson, & E. G. Hunt, 1952a, 1952b; W. A. Hunt, Wittson, & E. G. Hunt, 1954; Raines et al., 1954; Wittson, W. A. Hunt, & Stevenson, 1946) reported on a series of follow-up studies of recruits in three large U.S. Navy training centers who were evaluated for psychological problems. At the time of the initial evaluations, .7%, 2.6%, and 4.5%, respectively, of the selectees in the three centers were screened out for psychiatric problems; the corresponding figures for individuals discharged for this reason once on the job were 3.0%, 1.8%, and 1.5%. These data suggest that the more "at-risk" candidates are selected out early in an employment process, the fewer such discharges subsequently will be needed. It also appears that the percentage of candidates selected out will vary depending on the selection ratios (i.e., the size of the applicant pool compared with the number of positions to be filled). The base rate of rejection during World War II (when all manpower was needed for combat or support functions) was considerably lower than in the Korean conflict, when fewer were needed. More recently, Callan (1972) reported that between 10% and 20% of military recruits experience performance problems. Currently, the most extensive military screening takes place with enlisted recruits in the United States Air Force. Dr. Ed Gerwell (personal communication, December, 1988) estimates that the Air Force Medical Evaluation Test (AFMET) currently eliminates only about .75% of new trainees on the basis of psychiatric problems. However, about 7% of the recruits require more elaborate evaluation after an initial screening.

Three findings emerge from this early work. First, persons with mental health impairments were at higher

3

risk for difficulties on the job. Second, many individuals judged to be psychiatrically troubled performed their work effectively. Third, those not determined to be at risk at the time of the initial assessment were not immune from subsequent psychiatric problems. Concerning the second point, Egan, Jackson, and Eames (1951) studied a group of 2,054 men who had been rejected for service by their local Selective Service boards on the basis of neuropsychiatric reasons but who, for various reasons, subsequently served in the military nonetheless. Although 20.6% of this group were subsequently discharged from the Army for psychological reasons (including 5.6% for intellectual reasons), it is perhaps more noteworthy that almost 80% of the group served satisfactorily in the military.

Type of psychopathology appears to affect the propensity for and type of problems experienced on the job. Brill and Beebe (1952) found those with overt neuroses and personality disorders at the time of induction into the Army to be at highest risk for continued problems over time. The authors also noted that what they called "military stressors" (living in a controlled environment, etc.) were generally associated with the breakdown, and that the ability to withstand military stress declined with age. They concluded that "predisposition has been overgeneralized, and that we would do well to think more in terms of vulnerability to specific forms of stress and to the factors that may modify that vulnerability" (Brill & Beebe, 1952, p. 405).

W. A. Hunt, Wittson, and E. G. Hunt (1952a) reported that disciplinary cases were much more likely to come from those who had low intelligence or sociopathy or who were alcoholic than from those with neurotic or schizoid disorders. These researchers (1952a, 1954) found alcoholics and those with schizoid personalities to be especially likely to require hospitalization.

These early studies, largely neglected by current practitioners and researchers, provide a rich array of data about the base rate of psychopathology in applicant populations and about the ability of mentally disturbed individuals to work. They provide convincing evidence that, for males recruited from the general population, those assessed to have psychiatric problems at the time of employment are unquestionably at higher risk for subsequent psychological breakdown and/or failure on the job. However, the majority of those rated "at risk" appear to

4

be able to perform within acceptable standards, and sometimes in a superior manner, on the job. Blanket rejections cannot, on the basis of these studies, be supported, since there would be far too many false positives. Moreover, where the lines are drawn in rejecting candidates at risk of subsequent employment problems will vary depending on the selection ratios. Finally, there are differences in the rate of problems on the job depending on the type of pathology manifested and the extent of stressors on the job. Unfortunately, in these early studies little attention was paid to issues concerning the reliability and validity of the criteria used to establish impairment. Moreover, military populations in times of war or conflict may present issues not directly relevant to the practice of pre-employment screening in civilian populations. Nevertheless, these early studies are reasonably consistent with the results of newer research done with much more sophisticated screening devices.

GUIDELINES FOR PRACTICE

In practice, and regardless of the sufficiency of the validity base, psychologists today have increasingly been called upon to screen applicants for such potentially sensitive occupations as police, firefighters, transportation workers, and nuclear power plant operators. National advisory bodies have recommended, for example, that all police officers be subject to mandatory psychological screening prior to employment (e.g., *National Advisory Commission on Criminal Justice Standards and Goals: Police*, 1967). The Nuclear Regulatory Commission (1984, 1988) similarly has promulgated recommended guidelines for mandatory screening of candidates for employment. The intent in such screening programs is to identify those individuals who present significant risks of behavioral maladjustment on the job.

As in all areas of clinical practice, pre-employment screening for psychopathology is governed by a number of technical and ethical standards. The American Psychological Association's (APA's) (1981) Ethics Code provides a number of relevant principles. Also, the American Psychological Association's Ethics Committee (the group that reviews charges of ethical misconduct by psychologists) has provided case materials based on actual examples which illustrate the application of the ethical principles (see APA, 1982, 1983, 1984, 1987). Additional applications of these codes and guidelines to employment settings and issues have been published (e.g., London & Bray, 1980; Lowman, 1985; Mirvis & Seashore, 1979). Finally, other guidelines have been issued governing the application of psychology to specific issues. Most relevant here are the *Standards for Educational and Psychological Testing* (American Educational Research Association [AERA] et al., 1985), a cross-disciplinary set of standards promulgated jointly by the American Psychological Association, the American Educational Research Association, and the National Council on Measurement in Education.

While psychological screening of prospective employees represents a relatively new application of clinical and assessment psychology, the practice has become rapidly institutionalized, particularly in certain occupations regarded as being at high risk. The widespread promulgation of computerized testing techniques (Eyde & Kowal, 1987) has made the usage of certain psychological tests (especially the Minnesota Multiphasic Personality Inventory - MMPI) relatively easy and inexpensive. A number of testing firms have offered computerized pre-employment screening testing services, some directed to specific employee applicant groups such as police or firefighters. In addition, several venerable and emerging and existing tests have been suggested to be useful in pre-employment psychological screening for psychopathology (e.g., Aylward, 1985; Gruber, 1986; Inwald & Shusman, 1984b). These include the Bender Gestalt, the Eysenck Personality Inventory, the Fundamental Interpersonal Relations Orientation-Behavior (FIRO-B), the Shipley Institute of Living Scale, and the Symptom Checklist (Beutler et al., 1985); the California Personality Inventory (CPI) (Hargrave, 1985; Hogan, 1971; Pugh, 1985); the Inwald Personality Inventory (IPI) (Inwald, Knatz, & Shusman, 1982); the California Test of Personality, the Manson Evaluation, the Police Information Questionnaire, the Police Opinion Test, the Subjective History Questionnaire, and Vocational Fantasy Response (Aylward, 1985); and the Draw-A-Person Test (Rhead et al., 1968). (Excluded from review here are measures of normal personality used as predictors of successful job performance; e.g., Hogan et al., 1985.) To date, only three measures (the MMPI, the CPI, and the IPI) have much of a literature base specific to pre-employment screening for psychopathology.

While much activity is taking place in this area, there remains much uncertainty about appropriate standards for professional practice. This guide will therefore focus on four major issues: (a) validity of pre-employment psychological screening measures; (b) informed consent; (c) feedback to job applicants on the results of testing; and (d) advertising and marketing of psychological screening services. Each of these areas raises important ethical, legal, and professional practice concerns.

VALIDITY OF PRE-EMPLOYMENT PSYCHOLOGICAL SCREENING

Principle 8 of the APA's Ethical Standards (1981) addresses Assessment Techniques. The principle requires, among other things, that:

8b. Psychologists responsible for the development and standardization of psychological tests and other assessment techniques utilize established scientific procedures and observe the relevant APA standards.

8c. In reporting assessment results, psychologists indicate any reservations that exist regarding validity or reliability because of the circumstances of the assessment or the inappropriateness of the norms for the person tested. Psychologists strive to ensure that the results of assessments and their interpretations are not misused by others.

8e. Psychologists offering scoring and interpretation services are able to produce appropriate evidence for the validity of the programs and procedures used in arriving at interpretations. The public offering of an automated interpretation service is considered a professional-to-professional consultation. (APA, 1981, p. 637)

Also relevant are the *Standards for Educational and Psychological Testing* which, among other things, specify:

Standard 6.3. When a test is to be used for a purpose for which it has not been previously validated, or for which there is no supported claim for validity, the user is responsible for providing evidence of validity.

Standard 7.1. Clinicians should not imply that interpretations of test data are based on empirical

evidence of validity unless such evidence exists
for the interpretations given.

Standard 10.3. The rationale for criterion
relevance should be made explicit. It should include a description of the job in question and of
the judgments used to determine relevance.
(AERA et al., 1985, pp. 42, 46, 60)

These principles and standards appropriately require
that assessment devices be valid for their intended
purpose, in this case for screening out those individuals in
the applicant pool who are poor employment risks by
virtue of having certain types of psychological dysfunction. This personnel screening task is, essentially, a
"screen-out" process. The purpose is to identify and re-
move from further employment consideration those who
present a significant likelihood of manifesting aberrant
behavior which would interfere with performance on the
job.

The distinction between "screen-out" and "screen-in"
criteria requires clarification. Generally, the purpose of
screening for mental disturbance in an applicant pool is
to identify and eliminate from further employment
consideration those individuals who are sufficiently
psychologically impaired to constitute a *bona fide* risk to
the employer. In contrast, "screen-in" criteria refer to
those psychological characteristics that, if present, are
likely to be associated with positive outcomes; for
example, a pattern of abilities and interests shown to be
predictive of superior job performance. Some variables
can be *both* screen-out and screen-in criteria, depending
on the level of the variable present. For example, dominance in a candidate for a managerial position might be
associated with positive results if the individual scores in
a moderately high range, but might lead to negative
outcome if the assessee is at either extreme (i.e., overly aggressive or overly passive).

Clearly, the judgment that a variable constitutes a
"screen-out" criterion in pre-employment screening is not
to be made without literature support demonstrating
validity for the intended purpose. If, for example, a
psychologist recommends screening out employees who
have elevations above a certain T score on the MMPI on,
say, the Depression (2) scale, then there should be evidence supportive of this action. A clinician simply decid-

ing that depressed job applicants make (now or in the future) inadequate workers is insufficient.

"Screen-out" criteria require validity, just as do "screen-in" criteria. Meier, Farmer, and Maxwell (1987) mistakenly assume that screen-out methodologies require only that an instrument be able to describe behavior at the present time, not that the assessed behavior be predictive of future problematic behavior on the job. They state: "This [screen-out] process is more reliable and can be completed with greater validity" (p. 212). The description of psychopathology in the present is an easier and generally better-validated task than attempting to predict problematic behavior in the future on the basis of current conditions. Psychopathology in the present, however, is relevant in the employment selection process only if it has been demonstrated to place the assessee at higher risk of experiencing future job-related problems. By and large, this prediction task has shown a mixed record, as will be discussed in more detail below.

In general, it is rare that the same psychological screening measures will be valid for both "screen-out" and "screen-in" criteria. For example, the MMPI, the most commonly used screening device for assessing psychopathology of job applicants, measures the *presence* of psychopathology (which may or may not be associated with inferior job performance). With few exceptions, it does not measure the presence of so-called "desirable" characteristics such as cheerfulness, optimism, and so on. Moreover, in relation to the employment context, "screen-out" and "screen-in" measures must be validated separately for these purposes. There must be evidence that, when so used, the intended measure is valid as both a "screen-out" and "screen-in" device if used for both such purposes.

Consider, for example, the literature on "social intelligence" (Lowman & Leeman, 1988), or what is sometimes called "social cognition." From an occupational standpoint, there are probably minimal levels of interpersonal ability essential for employees to be able to get along with others on the job. Thus, someone impaired in the basic capacity to work cooperatively with others would be at a disadvantage in any job in which social interaction constitutes an important job dimension. A rather extensive literature exists (little of it, however, vocationally relevant), addressing the social skills of mental patients (for reviews of this literature, see Bellack & Morrison, 1982; Curran & Monti, 1982). However, this literature has very little to

say about the capacity of someone to function pro-
actively in a position for which interaction with others
constitutes a major dimension of successful performance
on the job. For example, sales personnel, teachers, psycho-
therapists, and managers all have important social/inter-
personal components in their work which at least theoreti-
cally require the presence of social skills. However, it is
not clear that social *dis*abilities encompass similar dimensions or variables as social abilities. Thus, absence of
social dysfunction (extreme shyness, inappropriate behavior in interacting with others, destructive or irrational
behaviors toward others) does not assure that one can
manage others effectively, positively motivate pupils'
behavior, or encourage someone to make a purchase. A
psychologist might "screen in" someone showing no major
social deficits who had insufficient interpersonal compe-
tencies to perform well on this job. Selection batteries
can be developed both for social skills and for social dysfunctions, but the psychologist certainly needs to be clear
on what is being measured in a particular selection assignment.

*TWO EXAMPLES: NUCLEAR
POWER PERSONNEL AND POLICE*

Unfortunately, in a guide of this length it is not
possible to review all the literature on pre-employment
screening for psychopathology. To delimit the literature
examined, two occupational groups that have received a
great deal of literature attention will be emphasized:
nuclear power personnel and police. The case of nuclear
power plant personnel, because it has received close
scrutiny on a national level (including the publication by
a national regulatory agency of recommended guidelines
for pre-employment psychological screening) provides an
important example of the issues involved in conducting
pre-employment screening for psychopathology.

Nuclear Power Personnel. Although the Nuclear
Regulatory Commission (which oversees nuclear power
applications in the United States) promulgated detailed
guidelines for psychological screening in 1984 (Nuclear
Regulatory Commission, 1984), these guidelines have yet
to be adopted as an official mandate. Very recently
(March 1988), the Nuclear Regulatory Commission published a revised policy statement concerning Nuclear

10

Power Plant Access screening (Nuclear Regulatory Commission, 1988). This, too, is a proposed policy, not yet formally incorporated into official or mandatory practice. However, each nuclear utility is required to file a security plan which, when accepted, becomes binding on the utility (P. E. Berghausen, personal communication, May 1987). A number of nuclear power facilities have adopted the 1984 Nuclear Regulatory Commission guidelines. Moreover, tens of thousands of would-be employees have been required to undergo psychological screening as part of the job application process for positions such as those in the nuclear power industry. These assessments have largely been directed to weeding out individuals with demonstrated or suspected psychopathology which would be suggestive of possible troubles on the job.

What Is Being Screened Out? Much of the difficulty in competently screening job applicants relates to the inadequacy and inconsistency of the criteria to be used for screening candidates out. As Christy and Rasmussen (1963, p. 541) note: "Information on explicit criteria of psychiatric effectiveness is essential for an effective assessment program." As an illustration of the problems in this area, Tables 1-3 (pp. 12-15) display a summary of various criteria that have been put forth by different authorities as grounds for exclusion from employment in nuclear power facilities.

Table 4 (pp. 16-17) shows similar criteria that have been generated for Peace Officers (police), an occupation obviously different from nuclear power operators but one that raises many similar concerns (and which will be discussed in more detail below). A review of these proposed criteria for pre-employment screening shows that: (a) while there is some overlap in the various characteristics or behaviors proposed for the nuclear power operators, there are also many unique items; (b) the likelihood of a single psychological instrument or interview being able to screen for all the behavior or characteristics on even one of these lists is extremely small; (c) some of these lists include both "screen-out" and "screen-in" criteria; (d) some lists identify specific forms of psychopathology that are unacceptable (e.g., mood swings) while others attempt to define problems behaviorally (e.g., "freezes or becomes incapacitated"); and (e) the job-related maladaptiveness of some of these factors is undemonstrated. There appears

TABLE 1: MENTAL HEALTH CRITERIA FOR EXCLUSION (U.S. NUCLEAR REGULATORY COMMISSION)*

Behaviors/characteristics to be screened out:

1. Argumentative Hostility Toward Authority

   Including such behavior as:

   > Refusing to comply with rules
   > Bending rules
   > Fighting with others on the job
   > Refusing to accept a supervisor's authority

2. Irresponsibility

   Including such behavior as:

   > Operating equipment carelessly
   > Being frequently tardy or absent from the job
   > Taking impulsive action
   > Playing pranks

3. Defensive Incompetence

   Including such behavior as:

   > Covering up mistakes
   > Failing to inform others of relevant information
   > Being reluctant to act without direct orders
   > Worrying excessively about radiation overexposure

4. Adverse Reactions to Stress

   Including such behavior as:

   > Becoming indecisive or incapacitated in emergency situations
   > Current chemical abuse or dependency

5. Emotional and Personal Inadaptability

   Including such behavior as:

   > Mood swings
   > Social isolation
   > Disorientation
   > Lack of appropriate emotional response
   > Active hallucinations or delusions
   > Extreme suspiciousness

*Source: U.S. Nuclear Regulatory Commission, Office of Nuclear Regulatory Research, 1984, pp. 16-17.

TABLE 2: MENTAL HEALTH CRITERIA FOR EXCLUSION (AMERICAN NATIONAL STANDARD, SECURITY FOR NUCLEAR POWER PLANTS)*

A partial list of behaviors/characteristics to be screened out:

• Use of nonprescribed narcotic or hallucinogenic drugs or excessive use of alcohol

• A history of mental illness or emotional instability that may cause a significant defect in the individual's judgment or reliability

• Reliability and stability shall be indicated by the results of a reliable and valid personality test or by other professionally accepted clinical assessment procedure administered by or under the supervision of a licensed psychologist or psychiatrist cognizant of this standard

---

*Source: Extracted from American National Standard, ANSI/ANS-3.3-1982, with permission of the publisher, the American Nuclear Society, 1982, pp. 10-11.

TABLE 3: MENTAL HEALTH CRITERIA SUGGESTED FOR EXCLUSION IN SELECTING NUCLEAR POWER PERSONNEL*

Behaviors and Behavioral Patterns Associated with Risks to Nuclear Facility Security**

A. Behavioral patterns suggestive of inability to appropriately respond to stressful or crisis situations:

    (1) Immediate or Short-Term Negative Reactions to Crisis Situations

    Includes:

        Freezes or becomes incapacitated
        Retreats from the situation
        Displays a startled reaction or begins crying

(2) Reactions to Long-Term Effects of Accumulated Stress

Includes:

Develops mood changes
Exhibits constant worrying
Complains of subjective feelings of tension
Exhibits decreased frustration tolerance

B. Behavioral Patterns Indicative of Generalized Emotional Instability

(1) Hostility to Authority

Includes:

Refuses to follow orders
Refuses to accept help from others
Does not follow appropriate chain of command
Becomes easily agitated

(2) Illegal and Antisocial Behaviors

Includes:

Steals from organization
Vandalizes facilities
Engages in sabotage
Intentionally provides inaccurate information to co-
workers and superiors

(3) Irresponsibility

Includes:

Is careless in performing duties
Is frequently tardy or absent
Appears unconcerned with disciplinary measures
Plays pranks on others on the job
Conducts personal business while on duty
Acts impulsively

(4) Dependent Behavioral Patterns

Includes:

Is overly fearful of radiation exposure when no real
danger is present
Is unable to make own decisions and needs explicit
instructions
Shows signs of extreme timidity on the job

(5)   Interpersonal Skill Deficiencies

Includes:

      Shows lack of proper assertion
      Tends toward social isolation or withdrawal
      Is unable to effectively transmit necessary information
      Stutters when trying to speak to others

(6)   Deficiencies in Vigilance

Includes:

      Displays low boredom tolerance
      Sleeps on the job
      Tries to create excitement

(7)   Emotional and Thought Disturbances

Includes:

      Shows no emotion at all
      Is overemotional (laughs, cries, becomes upset over minor things, etc.)
      Has insomnia
      Develops changes in appetite
      Appears disoriented in time and space
      Is quite forgetful and has memory lapses
      Displays recurrent mood swings, from severe depression to extreme euphoria
      Displays lack of attention to personal appearance
      Exhibits excessive suspiciousness
      Expresses sensory hallucinations
      Displays difficulty in comprehending and responding to questions
      Creates and uses meaningless words or phrases
      Displays emotional responses which are inappropriate to the situation
      Exhibits delayed reaction time
      Displays decline in intellectual functioning

---

*Source: U.S. Nuclear Regulatory Commission, Office of Nuclear Regulatory Research, 1981, pp. A-15 to A-18.

**The behavioral patterns listed here are illustrative excerpts; for the full listing of behaviors to be excluded, please see the source document.

TABLE 4: MENTAL HEALTH CRITERIA
(CALIFORNIA COMMISSION ON PEACE
OFFICERS STANDARDS AND TRAINING)*

Personality/behavioral attributes judged by peace officer supervisors
to be related to job performance:

1. Achievement

   Poor goal achievement

   Desired: Good goal achievement

2. Flexibility

   Excessive rigidity and conventionality

   Desired: Flexibility should be combined with recognition
   of the need for rules

3. Sensitivity

   Absence of paranoid-like hypersensitivity
   Insensitivity to others

4. Maturity

   Excessive need for attention, impulsivity, exaggeration

5. Intelligence

   Low intellectual functioning

   Desired: Average or high intelligence

6. Somatic Concerns

   Preoccupation with physical problems
   Excessive denial of problems

   Desired: Very few physical complaints

7. Mood

   Any deviation in mood, either depressed or manic-like

   Desired: Cheerful, optimistic mood

8. Social Adjustment

   Withdrawal, dependency, excessive shyness, or social awkwardness

   Desired: Outgoing, self-confident, assertive social poise

9. Anxiety

   Nervousness, fears, worries, and tenseness

   Desired: Presence of calm, relaxed, self-confident stance

10. Emotional Control

    Loss of emotional control, overcontrol, denial, intense anger

    Desired: Deliberate, calm, conforming, assertive posture

11. Dominance

    Inhibition, passivity, lack of confidence, overdominance

    Desired: Leadership, confidence, self-reliance

12. Moral-Ethical Behavior

    Average or below ethical behavior or "excessive" belief in "higher law"

    Desired: "Highly ethical" behavior

13. Impression Formation

    Making no effort to maintain a good impression; inability to sustain an initial good first impression

    Desired: Consistent ability to form average or good impression on others

14. Attitudes

    Extremely liberal attitude critical of restrictive rules

---

*Source: Adapted from Hargrave and Berner, 1984, pp. 33-36.

to be relatively little overlap between the proposed screening criteria and the variables typically employed by psychologists doing this work. There is little evidence that psychologists have validated the commonly used screening devices (such as the MMPI and interview) for the very specific behaviors suggested by these guidelines.

The MMPI, for example, demonstrates good validity for the measurement of certain categories of psychopathology (Greene, 1980). It has not been shown, however, to be related to behavior as specific as "freezes or becomes incapacitated" (Table 3, pp. 13-15) in a crisis at work in a nuclear power plant. Even if it were demonstrated that a job candidate had a high propensity to "freeze up," it is not clear that this behavior would necessarily occur both on and off the job; that is, that it constitutes a trait variable. If the most widely used (Parisher, Rios, & Reilley, 1979) pre-employment screening measure has not been validated against job criteria, it is even less likely that other psychological instruments (including the clinical interview) have been.

To further illustrate the problems with some of the criteria that have been proposed for the nuclear power industry, consider the screen-out criteria listed in Table 1 (p. 12). Probably few employers would disagree that the first two criteria listed constitute qualities to be avoided in potential employees, but the remaining three items are elaborated in a complex and rather inconsistent manner. For example, "Defensive Incompetence" includes "such behavior as covering up mistakes, failing to inform others of relevant information, being reluctant to act without direct orders, or worrying excessively about radiation overexposure." This hardly constitutes a cohesive grouping of behaviors or characteristics, and it is difficult to conceive a theory or test that would organize these behaviors together into a single category. Similarly, the category "Adverse Reaction to Stress" includes "indecisiveness or incapacitated in emergency situations" and "current chemical abuse or dependency." "Emotional and Personal Inadaptability" includes: "mood swings, social isolation, disorientation, lack of appropriate emotional response, active hallucinations or delusions, or extreme suspiciousness" (U.S. Nuclear Regulatory Commission, Office of Nuclear Regulatory Regulation Research, 1984, pp. 16-17), an assortment of seemingly diverse manifestations of moderate to extreme psychopathology.

Professionals therefore need to be clear on the specific criteria they are attempting to screen against and the validity, for these purposes, of the measures they are using. Thus, an early task for those who wish to practice ethically and professionally in screening applicants for psychological instability is to reach consensus on the screening criteria to be employed, and to communicate clearly to the contracting organization or employer whether screening methods to be used have demonstrated validity for the defined criteria, and with what exceptions and qualifications. At the least, practitioners need to define explicitly what criteria they have used as grounds for exclusion.

Moreover, screening criteria, like tests, require validity. Criteria must have credibility and justification, and not just be something that someone somewhere thought was a good idea. It must be demonstrated that the proposed screening criteria have obvious *prima facie* validity (e.g., employee theft) or that there is a relationship between the proposed criterion of psychopathology (e.g., depression) and problematic behaviors when on the job. For example, it might be easy to defend the inappropriateness of hiring an actively psychotic worker for a nuclear power plant; but what about an applicant, formerly alcoholic, with a 10-year history of sobriety, who still has an elevation on the MacAndrews Alcoholism (MAC) scale on the MMPI? Is someone manifesting sociopathic behaviors on a psychological test also likely to manifest these behaviors when at work? Unfortunately, in many cases, there is little evidence in the literature to support the on-the-job dysfunctionality of criteria proposed or used in pre-employment screening. Psychopathology *per se* is not a contraindication for employment. In fact, as will be discussed later, there is some indication that the majority of individuals with certain categories of psychological pathology may perform no worse (and in some cases, may do better) in certain occupations than those with normal profiles on psychological tests.

The absence of agreement on what constitutes problematic behaviors, or characteristics to be screened out or in, is a major problem in implementing consistent pre-employment screening policies throughout the country. With the present state of knowledge and practice, the same applicant could be accepted or rejected by the same psychologist using the same test(s), depending on what criteria and decision rules were employed. Some of the suggested lists of "screen-out" criteria are so comprehensive that it is difficult to imagine any applicants who would be acceptable. Moreover, Schoenfeld, Kobos, and Phinney (1980) showed that even experienced psychologists use markedly different strategies in reviewing the same MMPI data to make recommendations on employability. Hargrave (1985) presented somewhat more optimistic results when a larger sample of clinician raters was employed.

The absence of guidelines for making use of criteria is also problematic. Is a single "Yes" in a criterion list of 35 items grounds for rejection? If not, how many? Five, 10, half? Clearly, there is a need for reaching greater agreement, preferably on the basis of empirical findings, on which criteria should be "screened out" for a given selection task and with what order or priority. This is not to suggest that there is a need for a single list of such criteria for all jobs or levels of security clearance. However, an applicant for a similar nuclear power plant or police position in New York and in California, both required to be psychologically screened before employment should be assured that similar standards will be used in both settings to determine whether the individual will be judged unemployable on the basis of psychological problems. In the absence of such consensus, decisions will be made on the basis of unknown and unstated criteria. The result is likely to be unacceptably high variability from both a security and a legal perspective.

Without agreement on criteria and assessment patterns appropriate for screening out, a great deal of work in this area apparently is being conducted using generic screening devices, such as the MMPI, with no job-specific criteria. One commercially available computerized screening product, for example, the *Minnesota Personnel Interpretive Report*[TM], consists of a narrative MMPI report said to be useful in screening for personnel selection purposes. The computerized report (Butcher, 1983) has narrative paragraphs addressing several categories: Profile Validity, Personal Adjustment, Interpersonal Relations, Behavioral Stability, and Possible Employment Problems. A sample report contains such statements as: "The applicant is quite immature, self-oriented, and impulsive, and shows little regard for others . . . She may be hostile and aggressive toward others . . . She views her home situation as unpleasant and lacking in love and understanding . . . She is a rather unstable person who often

20

becomes embroiled in difficulties as a result of her personality problems. Her profile is quite stable, however, and not likely to change much over time" (Butcher, 1983, pp. 1-2).

One assumes that the characteristics ascribed to this (presumably hypothetical) applicant for a flight crew position would argue against hiring her. The evaluative statements were apparently generated on the basis (among other things) of an elevation (T score greater than 70) on the Pd (4) scale of the MMPI. While these statements may describe behavior generally valid in clinical populations, there is little evidence to show that the problematic behaviors generalize to the work situation or to non-clinical populations. It simply has not been demonstrated empirically that persons earning scores like this on the MMPI are likely to exhibit behavior as described when on the job. Although a variant of the validity-generalization hypothesis (Schmidt et al., 1985) might be argued (actually, a trait rather than situationally-specific view of psychopathology), to the effect that sociopathic tendencies as reflected by the MMPI generalize from personal life to the work setting, there is little empirical evidence on which to base such a hypothesis. To reject a job candidate on this many assumptions would not appear to be substantiated. Moreover, there is evidence that, at least for certain occupational groups, mild elevations on scales such as the Pd on the MMPI may actually be predictive of success on the job (see below).

Criteria used for pre-employment screening need to be defined by the employer and/or psychologist, measures selected to screen for these criteria must have demonstrated validity for that purpose, and that validity evidence (not one's guesses and hunches) should be used as the basis for differentiating among job candidates. Failing that, the psychologist will be in a very poor position for defending the appropriateness of the screening methods that were employed.

Validity of Psychological Tests for Pre-Employment Screening. Even if there were convincing evidence that criteria such as those discussed above constituted clear and unambiguous threats to employability (which in many cases they do not), there is little indication that the existing psychopathology-screening devices are well suited to determining the presence of these characteristics as they relate to employment. There is certainly no common agreement, based on a preponderance of empirical research evidence, about the specific pattern of test results that would constitute reasonable guidelines for exclusion or inclusion on these particular criteria.

Regulations proposed (but never formally adopted) by the U.S. Nuclear Regulatory Commission, Office of Nuclear Regulatory Research (1984), for example, stipulated a set of proposed minimal screening criteria and required, regardless of the criteria actually used, that each nuclear power plant licensee develop a list of the criteria to be used in pre-employment screening. The Nuclear Regulatory Commission also stipulated that the test of psychopathology "demonstrate validity in the form of statistical relationships between scores and behavior" (U.S. Nuclear Regulatory Commission, Office of Nuclear Regulatory Research, 1984, p. 18). The 1988 guidelines proposed by the Nuclear Regulatory Commission are less specific about how a relationship between predictor and criterion be demonstrated, putting the burden on "a licensed psychologist or psychiatrist" to attest to reliability and stability (Nuclear Regulatory Commission, 1988, p. 7537). Exclusionary criteria of the 1988 proposed guidelines include: "History of mental illness or emotional instability that may cause a significant defect in the individual's judgment or reliability" and "A psychological evaluation which indicates that the individual is a risk in terms of trustworthiness or reliability" (Nuclear Regulatory Commission, 1988, p. 7537). This approach puts the onus for proving validity onto the screening professional. Whatever criteria are employed, more than clinical judgment is needed: Validity must be demonstrated for the screening methodology employed.

An example of the complexity of practice issues raised by this work is provided by the MMPI. Unfortunately, there are many as yet unproved assumptions about the utility of the MMPI for personnel selection purposes. Most readers are aware that the MMPI was developed and standardized in the 1930s and 1940s using hospital inpatients. Despite this initial purpose (and to its credit, for purposes of validity), the MMPI has subsequently been used in thousands of studies covering many aspects of psychopathology in a very diverse array of patient treatment settings. However, despite a generally rich validity base, few studies have yet been published assessing the appropriateness of using the MMPI for employment screening purposes. Early studies attempting to use the MMPI for personnel selection purposes (reviewed by Guion & Gottier, 1965; Hedlund, 1965) were not promising.

Since the MMPI was never designed for selection purposes, it may or may not turn out to be appropriate for these methods. It is possible that the MMPI is an efficient selector of individuals at high risk for malfeasance or misbehavior on the job. It is also possible that it is not. An *a priori* assumption of validity cannot be made about the MMPI or any other measure not designed and validated against employment criteria. There simply is not a sufficient amount of published research evidence predicting to employment criteria to determine whether or not it is valid for these purposes. Stated another way, individuals may have established pathology on the MMPI (or any other screening device, including the clinical interview) and still perform appropriately on the job; or they may not. Only empirical studies, published in the professional literature to allow accumulation of knowledge, ultimately will determine the appropriateness and utility of pre-employment psychological screening devices.

There are, of course, many under-researched issues in mental health. Of particular concern in this case is the wide discrepancy between the use of pre-employment screening devices and the validity evidence supporting such use. Many implicit and explicit presumptions about the efficacy of these methods have gone unchallenged and unchecked. Yet the American Psychological Association's test standards are quite clear in stating: "When a test is to be used for a purpose for which it has not been previously validated, or for which there is no supported claim for validity, the user is responsible for providing evidence of validity" (AERA et al., 1985, p. 42).

In addition, even if there were agreement on criteria and predictors to be employed, there must be some empirical basis for the cut-off scores used to determine whether an applicant is to be rejected on the basis of the scores on psychopathological screening devices. For example, is a T score above 70 on one MMPI clinical scale sufficient grounds for rejecting an applicant? Are elevations on scales 5 (Masculinity-Femininity) or 9 (Mania, also associated with high energy levels) grounds for exclusion? If so, on the basis of what validity evidence specific to employment? If the results of the MMPI are merely reviewed by a clinician who will then, with or without a clinical interview, make a fitness-for-duty determination, by what standards should the clinician make this determination? What assurances of reliability exist among different clinicians doing the same work?

Illustrative of the problems in establishing rejection criteria are the results of a study by Lavin et al. (1987). Of 24 men in a nuclear power employment context (the Tennessee Valley Authority) referred because of observed behavioral difficulties on the job, there were clear differences on the MMPIs completed at the time of referral compared with the pre-employment MMPIs of individuals selected for employment. Group differences were found on eight scales: Infrequency (F), Hypochondriasis (1), Depression (2), Psychopathic Deviate (4), Paranoia (6), Psychasthenia (7), Schizophrenia (8), and Hypomania (9). All of the mean differences were higher for the "troubled employee" group than the referred group. However, *no average T score for the referred group was as high as 70*, the traditional cut-off score for indicating psychopathology. When it is further considered that the MMPIs for the referred group were completed at the time of the acute experience of the work difficulties, while the comparison group completed their MMPIs prior to employment, the ability of the MMPI (using traditional cut-off scores) to detect persons at risk for job disruption in employment contexts appears to be problematic.

The authors also examined the pre-employment MMPIs available for 8 of the 24 men subsequently referred. They found differences between the pre-employment MMPI and the normative group and between the pre-employment MMPI and those completed at the time of the supervisory referral. In each case, however, the MMPI scores were well below T scores of 70. None of these differences were statistically significant. However, 4 of the 8 referred employees had at least one MMPI scale score elevated $\geq$ 70 at the time of referral.

Police. More research has been conducted and published on the use of instruments like the MMPI in the selection of police and peace officers than for nuclear power operators, though the generalizability of findings from one occupational group to another may be problematic. (There may be systematic mean differences in occupational groups on instruments like the MMPI; see, for example, Daniels & Hunter, 1949; Verniaud, 1946. Other researchers have also pointed to systematic occupational differences in the experience of psychopathology; see Colligan, Smith, & Hurrell, 1977; Jamison, 1985; Lowman & Parker, 1988.)

Since Matarazzo et al.'s (1964) early work on characteristics of successful police and fire applicants, a number of studies on police populations have appeared. If a composite picture of police populations emerges from these studies, it is generally consistent with Matarazzo et al.'s early study suggesting an occupational group that is composed primarily of well-adjusted individuals who have narrow, traditional interests, who are reasonably bright (though this may be changing downward; see Burbeck & Furnham, 1985), and who have primarily Realistic and Investigative type vocational interests in Holland's (1985) interest typology. Similarly, Hogan (1971) found success in police training and on-the-job performance to be predicted by several variables on the California Psychological Inventory, especially Sociability (Sy), Self Acceptance (Sa), and Intellectual Efficiency (Ie). However, the predictors statistically associated with outcome measures were not consistent across his four samples. Only two scales on the CPI (Well Being [Wb] and Intellectual Efficiency [Ie]) predicted to both the training and the on-the-job performance criteria. Generally, the CPI was more strongly associated with the job performance than the training criterion, suggesting that there may be difficulty generalizing from studies done using training criteria to situations in which job-related performance criteria are important. In Hogan's studies, the best single predictor for the training criterion was Intellectual Efficiency (Ie), essentially a surrogate measure of intelligence (see Megargee, 1972), suggesting, as with IQ, that bright persons do better in training than do less bright ones. While the Ie scale predicted somewhat to the on-the-job criterion, it did not do so as strongly as the Achievement via Conformance (Ac) scale. This implies that, once on the job, intelligence may be less important than the ability to move ahead within a well-established framework of acceptable behavior.

More recent literature confirms the early work suggesting that, as a group, candidates for police average well within normal limits on measures of psychopathology and display less intra-sample variability than many normative groups (Carpenter & Raza, 1987; Mills & Bohannon, 1980; Saxe & Reiser, 1976). Of course, the test patterns may at least partly be depressed by a tendency to positive self-representation ("fake good"), an issue to be discussed in more detail later.

Although several studies have shown differences between applicants and general population norms, police applicant groups still average well below usual norms of pathology. Carpenter and Raza's (1987) study, for example, showed that the applicant pool had its highest scores on the Psychopathic Deviance (4) and Mania (9) MMPI scales, especially for women (who also had a scale elevation in the nonfeminine direction on the Masculinity-Femininity scale, scale 5). While well below traditional cutting scores ($T \leq 70$) for the presence of psychopathology, the elevations on the sociopathic scales (4 and 9) of the MMPI suggest that there may be a subclinical 4-9 profile associated with those who are attracted to law enforcement.

Perhaps the most impressive research yet conducted concerning police applicant screening appears in a technical report that summarizes an important research program evaluating the effectiveness of the MMPI and the California Psychological Inventory (CPI) for purposes of selecting peace officers (Hargrave & Berner, 1984). Although the studies reported by Hargrave and Berner may or may not generalize to other applicant populations (such as nuclear power plant operators), their work is extremely valuable for its comprehensiveness and because a predictive validity strategy was used. It also provides important information about individuals who constitute "false positives" in pre-employment screening.

Specifically, Hargrave and Berner's (1984) work examined the efficacy of the MMPI and the CPI for predicting training performance and attrition of police cadets. Although this work has not yet examined long-term predictive validity, Berner argues that the training period for police officers provides the best criteria data, since on-the-job police work is relatively autonomous and the supervisor often has much less information about actual performance than does a training instructor (J. G. Berner, personal communication, May 15, 1987). On the other hand, Hogan (1971) found higher associations between the California Psychological Inventory as a predictor for on-the-job ratings than for training criteria, suggesting the need to examine the results of these criteria separately.

The results of several studies, using both predictive and concurrent validity strategies, are reported by Hargrave and Berner (1984). Of 742 police cadets (all of whom had been screened before entering the program, but using background checks and additional methods other than psychological screening), 132 (17.8%) resigned from training before the completion of the program. Instructor ratings during the training were available for 479 individuals. An additional 110 subjects were followed up for 30 days in the field after completion of training. Some training groups took the MMPI, some the CPI, and one group completed both measures. All cadets also completed the Law Enforcement Attitudes Questionnaire. All of the measures were completed during the first week of training. The results of these tests were not revealed to the candidates or to their instructors. Three clinical psychologists, all said to be experienced in such work, evaluated the personality test data and made an independent recommendation on whether the candidate was Acceptable, Marginal, or Unacceptable on the basis of the test results. Peer and supervisory ratings were collected that evaluated the overall effectiveness of the candidates for police work.

Regarding attrition, the MMPI results correctly classified 73% of those cadets who dropped out of the training. The California Psychological Inventory correctly classified 67%. The sample completing both the MMPI and the CPI had a correct classification rate of 73%. A Behavior Rating Scale (BRS) was completed for many in the study. This form recorded the instructors' ratings of performance and overall fitness for police work. Three criterion groups were established: those who completed the program with average or above-average BRS ratings, those who completed the program with below-average BRS ratings, and those who dropped out of the program. Using a criterion on the MMPI of one or more T-score elevations equal to or greater than 70, the authors grouped individuals into four categories: those with elevations on one or more of the "Anxiety scales," those with "Psychotic scale" elevations, those with "Personality Disorder scale" elevations, and those with "subclinical" profiles (i.e., no MMPI-demonstrated pathology). Of the 293 subjects included in this analysis, 28% had abnormal MMPI profiles while 72% were within normal limits. Of those with abnormal profiles, 45% completed the training with BRS ratings at the average level or above, 39% dropped out, and 16% completed the training with a low BRS rating. Of the subclinical profile group (n = 211), 65% completed the training program successfully, 21%

dropped out, and 15% completed the program with a low BRS rating.

Among the groups manifesting signs of pathology on the MMPI, there were between-group differences when individuals were classified by type of MMPI elevation. Those with high scores on the so-called "neurotic" scales dropped out at the highest rate; only one of the 11 cases successfully completed the program. Of those ($n = 44$) with "psychotic" scale elevations (in which the authors included elevations on the Hypomania scale, 9), 45% completed the program successfully, 36% dropped out, and 18% completed the program with low ratings. Finally, for the personality-disordered group, 59% (of the 27 in this category) successfully completed the program, 30% dropped out, and 11% completed the program with low ratings (Hargrave & Berner, 1984, p. 47).

It can be concluded from these studies that: (a) those with elevated (T scores $\geq$ 70) MMPI profiles are at higher risk of dropping out of a police training program or of completing it with lower ratings; (b) a significant percentage of individuals with MMPI-defined pathology, especially those with MMPI-defined personality disorders, can successfully complete police training; and (c) type of psychopathology appears to moderate one's ability to perform well in an employment context. These findings are open to various interpretations. It should be noted that the authors present their findings as evidence supporting the validity of the MMPI for personnel-screening applications. On the other hand, the number of false positives, especially for those with personality disorders, is of great concern. Clearly, longer-term research is needed to determine whether these individuals perform as successfully on the job as the majority did in the training. If so, psychologists may need to rethink the idea that any MMPI scale elevation above 70 predicts dysfunctionality at work.

It is not possible here to review all of the findings of Hargrave and Berner's important research (which has now begun to appear in the professional literature; e.g., Hargrave, 1985; Hargrave & Hiatt, 1987). However, one additional result from the original report will be noted. The authors plotted the maximum scale scores on the MMPI scales for a group of 178 incumbent officers already on the job, and compared the results with the maximal scores on the MMPI scales for 299 cadets in training who had not been selected on the basis of using the

MMPI. The maximal MMPI profiles of the two groups were demonstrably different (MMPI-screened incumbents lower), suggesting that the extremes of psychopathology may be eliminated by a pre-employment screening program. However, the *average* scores of the two groups were very similar - all subclinical.

When the maximal scores of cadets entering training were compared with the maximal scores of the 223 cadets completing the program, there was a very large difference in the profiles (the group completing the training had lower maximal scale scores), suggesting that extremely high scores on the MMPI place one at risk for attrition. On the other hand, the maximal scores for individuals rated highest in "emotional suitability" by their instructors and peers (n = 29) showed a clinical elevation above 70 on the Ma (9) scale and near-clinical elevations on the Pd (4) and Sc (8) scales of the MMPI. Furthermore, the *average* MMPI scores of the group rated highest by their instructors in emotional stability showed a subclinical elevation on the K and Ma (9) scales (T-score approximately = 60), and a clear low score on scale Si (0), results all more extreme than those rated lowest in emotional suitability (n = 19). These findings suggest that Ma (9) scale elevations and Si (0) low scores must be much more carefully researched in the employment setting to determine the extent to which they predict success, not failure, on the job. Similarly, subclinical elevations on the K scale of the MMPI may also be a positive predictor.

Summarizing, Hargrave and Berner's work provides important preliminary evidence for the usefulness of psychological tests of personality in police selection, at least predicting to a training criterion. Tests like the MMPI may be effective in weeding out persons at higher risk for attrition and poor performance. However, a significant minority, and in some cases majority, of those individuals with MMPI-defined psychopathology were successful in meeting job-related criteria. This suggests the need for more research to determine the types of psychopathology that are problematic on the job and those that are not dysfunctional. Until this happens, the use of automatic cut-off scores on the MMPI at a level of, say, T-scores of 70, appears to result in an unacceptably high number of false positives.

Other researchers have also examined the effectiveness of the MMPI and alternative screening devices as predictors of various job criteria in police settings.

Costello, Schoenfeld, and Kobos (1982) presented data in support of a new MMPI scale (the Goldberg Index) to differentiate acceptable and unacceptable police officers. Bartol (1982) reported that police officers rated as poorer in job performance tended to score significantly higher on scales K, Pd (4), M-F (5), Pa (6), and Ma (9). Inwald, who is the author of a psychological screening device for police selection purposes, has published various studies evaluating the effectiveness of such measures as the California Psychological Inventory and the MMPI compared to her own measure, the Inwald Personality Inventory (IPI). Shusman, Inwald, and Landa (1984) compared the MMPI and the IPI as predictors of police who manifested poor work performance ($\geq$ 3 times absent or late; referral for disciplinary interviews) or who were terminated in their first year of service. However, all applicants had been screened using psychological measures and some candidates were rejected on the basis of psychological evaluation procedures, creating a problem of restriction in range.

The discriminant function equations in this study generated separately and conjointly for MMPI and IPI raw scores were reported to correctly classify group membership from 63% to 73% of the officers who were discharged or terminated (n = 51 terminated vs. n = 665 retained). Similar results were found with the other criterion variables (lateness or absenteeism $\geq$ 3 times or disciplinary actions) for both validation and cross-validation samples. The authors reported that no MMPI scales discriminated between individuals retained and terminated on the job, while absences were predicted only by the MAC Scale and lateness by the MAC, Frequency (F), M-F (5), and Paranoia (6) scales of the MMPI. The MAC, F, and Pd (4) scales of the MMPI were also significantly different (all higher) for those individuals who had disciplinary interviews than for those who did not. Similar results are also reported by Inwald and Shusman (1984b).

Unfortunately, no information was provided in these studies outlining the criteria employed by the psychologists who weeded out applicants using, in part, the MMPI and the IPI, and no raw or standardized score profiles of the clinical scales for the various groups were provided. Moreover, Shusman et al. (1984) noted, in describing the validation and hold-out samples, that 24% of the former and 18% of the latter had been arrested at least once,

30

possibly suggesting a rather deviant police group from which generalizability would be difficult. Thus, this research is contaminated in that applicants (a) were selected partly on the basis of the MMPI and the IPI; and (b) were possibly atypical of other police applicant pools in that, despite the pre-selection criteria, many of those selected to be police officers had prior arrest records. Finally, the authors of this research conclude that the measure they developed (the IPI) was a superior police screening tool to the MMPI. However, several of the IPI scales (e.g., Antisocial Attitudes and Substance Abuse) that the authors reported to have differentiated better than the MMPI among the criterion groups did not have a pattern of prediction similar to analogous MMPI scales (e.g., the MAC scale). That a similar pattern of prediction was not found as on the much more extensively validated MMPI may suggest that the IPI, regardless of its predictive power, is measuring constructs or characteristics different from the labels attached to the scales by the test authors.

Muha and May (1973) used MMPI scores and demographic variables to predict to clinical-interview established ratings of fitness or unfitness for work at a federal government agency. They found that the use of multiple regression equations helped identify job applicants with impairing emotional problems. Their regression equations differed by sex. The following variables (for the MMPI scales only) were included in the regression equation for females [L, -K, Hs (1), -D (2), Pd (4), Pa (6), Pt (7), -Ma (9)] and for males [F, -K, Hs (1), Pt (7), -Ma (9), -Si (0)].

Evans (1976) used the MMPI to develop a special scale to predict which crisis-intervention telephone workers would be conscientious in their work. This scale was reported to classify 83%-92% of individuals correctly, and specific regression equations were offered. In predicting to success on the job for police officers, Azen, Snibbe, and Montgomery (1973) found the MMPI to predict six job-related criteria for a group of 95 Los Angeles County sheriffs who had been on the job for 20 years. Both the MMPI Ma (9) scale (directly) and the D (2) scale (inversely) predicted to the criterion of number of automobile accidents. Sacuzzo, Higgins, and Lewandowski (1974) reported on the use of the MMPI and a measure of interests (Kuder) and intelligence (Otis-Lennon) to select police officers. They found that the mean MMPI profiles of police officers had no scales above 60, that K scores aver-

31

aged about 58, and that the modal high point scores (all below 60, on average) were on the MMPI Pd (4), Hy (3), and Ma (9) scales.

Not all studies have been as supportive of the use of the MMPI and similar measures in pre-employment screening contexts. Guion and Gottier (1965) reviewed five studies of the use of the MMPI in industrial contexts. Though this review was not unflawed (Hogan et al., 1985), they generally found little association between MMPI scores and employment outcomes such as job satisfaction. Truck drivers' accidents were predicted by four MMPI scales: Ma (9), Hs (1), Mf (5), and Pt (7). Similarly, Hedlund's review of the uses of the MMPI in industry (Hedlund, 1965) was generally pessimistic about its utility for job-related prediction. Arvey, Mussio, and Payne (1972) reported that for 11 dimensions of job performance, the MMPI predicted only to flexibility on the job. Using a concurrent validity model, Schoenfeld et al. (1980) found that the MMPI did not differentiate between officers rated unacceptable and those rated more positively. Burbeck and Furnham (1985) reviewed the literature on the MMPI and other personality screening devices (though they overlooked many important studies), and concluded that the MMPI was not very helpful as judged by the validation literature. Hargrave and Berner (1984) provide a comprehensive listing of much literature on pre-employment screening of police; their review includes many studies not readily accessible in the professional literature. Since space limitations in this guide do not permit a comprehensive literature review, the interested reader is referred to Hargrave and Berner's document for a more comprehensive overview of the police selection literature.

Summary. What this series of articles suggests is that pre-employment measures have generally shown a mixed pattern of results when used to predict to job-related criteria as opposed to those criteria more narrowly associated with psychopathology. Except for variables such as introversion and energy level, measures like MMPI generally assess aspects of behavior or personality which have not yet proven clearly to be associated with work-outcome criteria. Tests of psychopathology have at least some validity for purposes of weeding out individuals with mental dysfunctions who will be at higher risk of performing poorly in training or on the job, though at the not insignificant cost of many false positives. However, tests do not appear to predict beyond that to such multidimensional constructs (which have little theoretical relationship to psychopathology) as job satisfaction, high job performance, and good interpersonal relationships on the job. At best, pre-employment psychological screening will screen out persons whose mental dysfunctions may impair work performance. However, it cannot be concluded that all types of psychopathology are equally problematic in the workplace.

IMPORTANT, UNRESOLVED ISSUES

Several other issues are also important to consider in doing pre-employment psychological screening.

Does Psychopathology Interfere with Job Performance? The literature reviewed thus far raises the important issue of whether persons meeting the traditional criteria for psychopathology necessarily manifest problems in their work. Most psychologists would probably agree, for example, that an acutely psychotic individual is not suited at that time for employment in a nuclear power plant or police force. On the other hand, there are many types of psychopathology whose effect on work performance has not been established, and which may not be job disruptive.

For the two occupational groups (police and nuclear power personnel) highlighted here, the literature presents a mixed picture of the validity of pre-employment screening devices. Most studies have shown that applicant groups *on average* present well within normal limits on traditional cut-off scores for establishing psychopathology. Two groups present special problems: Studies have typically found that many in the rather small group of persons manifesting later on-the-job problems do not present with evidence of psychopathology at the time of screening; secondly, a not-insignificant number of persons scoring "positively" on screening measures have been shown to perform adequately or even well on the job.

The assumption that certain varieties of psychopathology necessarily will impair job performance has generally not been proved. For example, Sutker and Allain (1983) compared eight male medical students who met the criterion for sociopathy on the MMPI with eight

MMPI-defined normal medical students. Although the MMPI-sociopaths acknowledged having had greater adolescent deviance, and having more personal problems, they were not shown to have problems in their ability to relate to others or in their work performance. The authors hypothesize that vocational rewards may serve as mediators of maladaptive behaviors. Stated another way, it is possible that a person might be sociopathic as defined by the MMPI and still progress well on the job. Indeed, some would argue that sociopathy is a prerequisite for advancement in many settings.

The last statement is not entirely facetious. In a study (T. W. Harrell, 1972; T. W. Harrell & M. S. Harrell, 1973) of MBA students who reached general management earlier than their peers, the successful general managers and higher-earning MBAs were found to have somewhat elevated MMPI scores (compared to consultants, accountants, and marketing consultants) on the following MMPI scales: Pd (4), Pa (6), and Ma (9). They scored lower than accountants on the Si (0) scale. This may imply that, at least in some occupations, high energy, coupled with absence of social introversion and presence of some degree of suspiciousness or sociopathy, may be adaptive. On the other hand, while higher than other MBA groups, the scale scores of the more successful MBAs were still subclinical. Hogan et al. (1985) also point to "a general trend for better employee performance to be associated with higher scores on some measures of deviance" (p. 32).

The consistency with which the Ma (9) and Pd (4) scales appear in the MMPI literature related to police and some other occupational groups is striking. It is possible that so-called character pathology, at least at subclinical, or mild, levels of elevation, may in the work setting be adaptive rather than dysfunctional. Gynther, Altman, and Warbin (1973), for example, reported that an inpatient group of persons with elevations on the Pd (4) and Ma (9) scales of the MMPI did not meet the presumed characteristics ascribed to them in the MMPI literature and did not hold up in a replication study. Scales Pd and Ma, at least for police populations, may constitute both "screen-out" and "screen-in" criteria, depending on the level of elevation. Individuals may need a certain amount of elevation (presumably subclinical) on these scales to successfully perform the job, but when a certain point is reached (and this point may well be higher than a T score of 70), the characteristics may be dysfunctional. These findings may apply only to certain career choices such as law enforcement, the military, and possibly certain aspects of management. Thus, the presence of test-defined psychopathology cannot be presumed to be related only negatively to job performance.

Situational Factors. It must also be questioned whether the results of a pre-employment MMPI may artifactually differ from post-employment results. Situational factors have been demonstrated to affect test results. For example, Masahiko et al. (1983) reported on the results of MMPI given during and after the entrance examination for medical school. The profiles for the same candidates were quite different before and after the examination. Specific to the nuclear power industry, Sajwaj, Ford, and McGee (1987) found statistically significant differences between employees in a licensed nuclear facility and those in one applying for its operating license. The former employee group was reported to be less stressed (though higher in Type A behavior), more involved in work, and significantly lower on interpersonal hostility. While it could be argued that the screening procedures used in the licensed plant resulted in superior employees, it is equally plausible that participating in an ongoing, important, and active enterprise is more psychologically healthful than simply waiting for a new facility to go operational. The *situation* rather than the work may well be the cause of the differences reported.

For How Long Is a Psychological Screening Measure Valid? The utility of psychological screening devices for predicting problematic behavior on the job is not indefinite. Persons may be certifiably "disease free" at the time of their application to a job and subsequently develop serious mental problems. Lavin et al. (1987) presented data from the TVA indicating a base rate of .7% (64 referrals out of 8,800 employees) of employees who required psychological re-evaluation. Of those referred, 73% were re-certified as being psychologically fit. Of the 64 referred, 34% had alcohol- or drug-related problems, 41% had affective disorders, and the rest experienced psychotic or personality disorders or were reported as having no psychiatric diagnosis. These results suggest that (a) even carefully screened employees can develop mental problems after the screening; and (b) therefore, a

35

requirement may be appropriate, at least in security-sensitive industries like nuclear power, that there be an ongoing behavioral monitoring program even after pre-selection screening (e.g., American Nuclear Society, 1982).

The Base Rates of Applicant Impairment and Rejection. Rather little published literature exists examining the base rate of rejection associated with pre-employment screening measures. Few studies have been published indicating the number of applicants with scale score elevations on the screening measures. Butcher (1979), employing a criterion of elevation on the clinical scales above a T score of 70 along with "valid" (never defined operationally) validity indicators, found that 18% of the females and 22.2% of the males in a sample of 1,726 job applicants had one or more clinical scales elevated. However, the most frequent elevation for both men and women was on the Ma scale, whose problems in this context have already been discussed. In addition, these figures included applicants with elevations on the Mf scale (5), a scale of questionable relevance to employment. Berner estimated that the California highway patrol currently eliminates about 15% of the applicants on the basis of psychological unfitness (personal communication, J. G. Berner, May 15, 1987). Brill and Beebe (1952) reported that 20% of a group of Caucasian inductees were determined in mental health screening to be "at risk." They compare this to a similar figure for World War II of around 12%. Rhead et al. (1968) reported that during an 18-month period screening applicants for Chicago police, 30% (of over 1,000 applicants) were recommended for further screening by a board of mental health professionals. Of the 30%, 20% (6% of the original sample) were judged to have "grossly incapacitating illness." All of these findings can be compared to national probability studies which estimate that 19%-20% of the general population is sufficiently impaired to merit a psychiatric diagnosis (National Institute of Mental Health, 1985). About 1% of the overall population would be included in these figures due to serious cognitive impairments. Procedures that result in more than 20% of an applicant population being rejected on mental health grounds may therefore be using overly stringent criteria for screening.

Use of Multiple vs. Single Measures to Screen Applicants. Some (e.g., Anastasi, 1984; Berghausen, 1985; Inwald, 1985) have advocated that psychological screening measures should ordinarily be combined with clinical interviews to improve validity. While the guidelines put forth by the Nuclear Regulatory Commission have argued for interviewing only those who would otherwise be screened out by the MMPI results, several psychologists have maintained that validity in screening out inappropriate candidates would be enhanced by use of both an objective instrument like the MMPI and a clinical interview for all candidates. This argument holds that a number of individuals ("false negatives") will show no signs of psychopathology on the MMPI but will demonstrate problematic behavior when interviewed. In addition, it is held, false positives may also be captured by the clinical interviewer.

It is likely, but empirically unestablished, that a certain number of false negatives will be captured by this methodology. However, the number of such individuals will vary depending on who is conducting the clinical interview and the extent to which there are defined and agreed-upon standards established for conducting the interviews (see, e.g., Schmitt, 1976). Moreover, there is also a risk (the extent of which is also unestablished empirically) of increasing the number of "false positives"; that is, the number of candidates for selection who are judged, inappropriately, on the basis of the clinical interview to be unsuitable for employment for psychological reasons. Finally, the cost of such interviews (which cynics might consider to constitute a "psychologists' employment act") must be balanced against likely employment savings to be made from conducting them. Again, this is not to say that use of the clinical interview is inappropriate or that validity would not potentially be improved by combining objective personality measures and interview data. Rather, once again there is insufficient empirical literature to determine if the presumed added validity is worth the costs (not to mention the possibility of added invalidity).

Use of Cut-Off Scores in Screening. In the absence of validity evidence or expert consensus, providers of pre-employment screening services will make decisions using their own criteria and cut-off rules. It would appear that there are considerable differences in the numbers of candidates accepted and rejected by various selection methods (Berghausen, personal communication, May 1988) even using the same instrumentation. The same candidate could be assessed by two different vendors of psychological screening using the same psychological instrumentation, and two very different conclusions could be reached about fitness for employment. Vendor A, for example, might use the MMPI and establish as a cut-off point any elevation on the clinical scales on the MMPI above a T-score of 70 in protocols with L below a T-score of 60 and K below a T-score of 70. Vendor B might adopt a more conservative stance, using higher threshold values for cut-off, and might also only use certain clinical scales (not, for example, single-point elevations on the Ma or Mf scales).

Clinical assessment for purposes of employment suitability should not be the place for creative interpretation and so-called clinical judgment in the absence of a demonstrated relationship to employability. Providers of psychological screening services have an ethical obligation to define explicitly the criteria that they have used to make judgments about employability. One hopes that they would also assume the responsibility for conducting or sponsoring the research needed to determine whether the methods they employ are valid. At least in the published literature, this has not yet happened.

What cut-off scores should the clinician use in practice? Regrettably, this question cannot reliably be answered on the basis of current literature. Although it will result in excessive "false positives," clinicians would probably be advised to interview and/or further assess candidates who, on the MMPI, have any T score above 70 except for the Mf (5) scale or Si (0) scale. Tests judged invalid (typically those with defended test-taking orientation) might also suggest the need for additional screening. Unfortunately, there is little basis for validly determining which cut-off score on validity indices should be employed. Borofsky's (1987) guidelines and recommended assessment methodologies have an aura of exactness that would not appear to be supported by extensive validation research. In the absence of employment-specific studies, practicing clinicians may need to use traditional criteria for test invalidity as the basis for determining the need for further assessment. In the employment context, however, this will result in a number of cases requiring further assessment.

Is Using Imperfectly Valid Psychological Screening Measures Better than Not Screening at All? It has been argued that, in the interests of security and safety (among other reasons) and in the absence of research suggesting invalidity, psychologists should use the best "broad-brush" instruments available to make pre-employment decisions. This argument was well stated by Meehl (cited in Butcher, 1979, pp. 191-192): "if a high degree of judgement and responsibility is required in the position for which you're screening and if your selection ratio is running reasonably small, then you should give [an MMPI] . . . [W]hen I fly, I would feel more comfortable knowing that some screening of the crew, even with imperfect tests, has been done--I would prefer not having 49's at the helm." But Meehl also stated: "if you are an industrial psychologist using the MMPI in the airline industry, you ought to try to validate it." Considering that Meehl's comments were originally published in 1969, the paucity of validation research on industrial uses of these tests - compared to the number of screening decisions based at least in part on psychological tests - becomes a much greater concern.

SUMMARY AND RECOMMENDATIONS: VALIDITY

At present, the validity of psychological pre-employment screening devices for screening out job candidates who will later have behavioral problems in the work setting is insufficiently established. Urgently needed in the published literature are more studies establishing the utility of psychopathological screening methods for employment purposes with diverse occupational groups. We need to know that proposed screening criteria for eliminating candidates from further employment consideration are work-related, and that the screening methods being used are validated for the intended task. Such research would, at a minimum, require collecting data on the pre-employment screening psychological profiles of those who, for one reason or another, are hired and subsequently experience behavioral problems on the job that are disruptive of their work. We also need to know what patterns of test scores and/or clinical interview results are associated with on-the-job behaviors of predictable types. Ideally, predictive validity studies would also be undertaken. Because the question of validity is of great relevance to employers, hopefully industry-wide consortia - sponsored by such industries as nuclear power

39

and police - could fund an ongoing research effort to examine these questions over time. This could provide a sufficiently large sample size to assure validity generalizability.

RECOMMENDATIONS FOR
FUTURE VALIDITY STUDIES

A careful reading of the literature suggests the need for much more research to clarify and extend some current findings. Future validation efforts would benefit from a greater degree of theorizing prior to conducting empirical validation studies. Researchers need to specify a rationale as to why certain patterns of psychopathology would be expected to interfere with job performance, and to differentiate between transitory situational disturbances and more ingrained patterns of behavioral disturbance. At this stage of research efforts, it cannot be assumed that psychopathology alone (or scoring above certain levels on psychological tests) is a contraindication to employment. At best, in evaluating fitness for employment, present psychological screening methods should be used as adjunctive data that will be combined with other information about a candidate. Of special interest, given the fairly large number of "false positives," is the need to protect the rights of those who would be excluded from employment on the basis of the psychological screening, yet who would perform well once on the job. Because very little research has been done on the work behavior over time of those who present with elevations on traditional measures of psychopathology, caution must be used in rejecting candidates for selection solely on the basis of psychological screening.

The research needed to demonstrate at least minimally acceptable validity is not without cost but, by this date, its appearance in the published literature is long overdue. Predictive studies may be difficult to implement because of possible security or safety risks. However, it is not difficult to retrieve psychological test results of individuals who exhibit problem behaviors after being hired. No such reports relating to nuclear power plant personnel, and very few pertaining to police, were found. An insufficient number of studies exists to establish reliable base rates on the number of candidates expected to be bad risks for employability when using various tests and criteria.

On the basis of the current literature, a number of suggestions can be made for those who plan to conduct research to determine the validity of pre-employment screening methods.

Response Bias. William Whyte, in *The Organization Man* (1956), advised job candidates on "how to cheat on personality tests." Because he felt that measures of personality for employment were of questionable validity, if not an intrusion into personal privacy, he advocated positive self-presentation and intentional "faking good" on personality screening measures. Whyte's advice may have been unnecessary (or else well followed), since there is a strong tendency to positive self-presentation on such tests.

Pre-employment screening measures that include validity indicators (e.g., the MMPI and CPI) generally find elevations on the "fake good" scales. Butcher (1979) reported that 8.6% of males and 6.8% of females, in an applicant sample of 1,403 males and 323 females, were invalid. Saxe and Reiser's (1976) sample of 296 Los Angeles Police Department applicants had a mean elevation on the K scale of 19.58 (T = 64) and 20.58 (T = 66) for a successful applicant group (n = 100). Interestingly, less successful applicant groups and applicants accepted but prematurely terminated had lower scores on the K scale (i.e., were less defended) though they were still higher than the normative group. Hargrave, Hiatt, and Gaffney (1986) found elevations in the "defended" direction for traffic officers and sheriffs' deputies who were rated high compared to those who were rated low, though the differences were small. These studies suggest, among other things, that the consistent literature finding that such groups as police are well within normal limits on the various screening measures used may at least partly be artifactual to test-taking "set." On the other hand, the ability to favorably self-present may be important in success on the job.

Individuals who know they are being evaluated for purposes of employment tend naturally to present themselves in the most favorable light. Butcher (1985) has argued that the person who does not self-present positively may be especially problematic on the job, and Hogan et al. (1985) also noted a "modestly consistent" association of the "fake good" response set with good on-the-job performance. However, few research data exist to address the specific meaning of test-taking set in the employment context. Whether or not validity indicators can be interpreted in the same manner as with clinical populations has not been adequately researched, particularly against job-related criteria. Although further research needs to be done on the meaning and implication of response set in the pre-employment screening, it is important that measures selected for use in this work have well-established indicators of response "set." Establishing the professional practice implications of validity indicators at different levels of elevation is an early, important research task.

Validity Generalization vs. Occupational Specificity. Contrary to the job-validity generalization hypothesis (i.e., that tests are valid across diverse settings and do not need situation-specific validation), occupational differences in the presence of psychopathology appear to complicate the norming process and, therefore, such issues as establishing appropriate cut-off scores. Because the experience of psychopathology varies from one occupational group to another, the idea that predictors and cut-off scores will have the same meaning across occupations does not appear to be well grounded. In some occupations, for example, it may be normative rather than deviant to experience psychopathology. There may actually be something adaptive about psychopathology in certain occupational pursuits. Poets and actors are two examples of occupational groups in which psychopathology may be expected and represent characteristics desirable for successful performance of the job. In other occupations, of course, psychopathology may be dysfunctional and may constitute appropriate grounds for exclusion.

Intra-group occupational differences must also be considered. Police, for example, do not constitute a unidimensional group. Group characteristics have been shown to vary with specific job duties (e.g., traffic officer vs. deputy sheriff) and the location and size of city in which the police force is based, among other variables (Bartol, 1982; Burbeck & Furnham, 1985; Carlson, Thayer, & Germann, 1971; Carpenter & Raza, 1987; Hargrave et al., 1986).

Issues with Predictors. Which predictors are most appropriately used for pre-employment screening? This question remains unanswered. Though the MMPI is by far the most widely used screening measure for at least some occupational groups (such as police), its prediction record is not necessarily the best. Especially troubling for all measures is the lack of consistency of the "successful" predictor variables from one sample or study to the next.

Some studies have used a psychological screening measure as the basis for choosing individuals, and then have attempted to validate the same measures against subsequent on-the-job performance. Shusman, Inwald, and Knatz's (1987) study, for example, compared the job performance of police recruits who had been selected, in part, on the basis of the MMPI and the IPI. However, this is a flawed method for determining the validity of pre-employment screening measures because of the restriction in range problem (the worst candidates were presumably eliminated on the basis of the test performance), and because persons conducting follow-up evaluations may not always have been oblivious to the results of testing. While not all studies can use predictive-validity paradigms, those that do (e.g., Hargrave & Berner, 1984) provide much more convincing tests for determining validity and utility. Predicting to job criteria over time provides a much more rigorous test than simply predicting at one point, because there are fewer restrictions in the range of scores when using a predictive-validity approach.

In clinical practice, it is customary to use both nomothetic and ideographic measures before assigning diagnoses to individuals (e.g., an MMPI *and* an interview) (Anastasi, 1984; Berghausen, 1985). Many aspects of behavior are better captured by face-to-face observation than by paper-and-pencil instrumentation (Wiens & Matarazzo, 1983). However, the utility of clinical interviews for predicting to job criteria has not yet been conclusively demonstrated. Although Berghausen (1985) argues that all job applicants receiving clinical screening should be interviewed, no such *a priori* assumptions can be made on the basis of the present literature. If, for example, objective paper-and-pencil measures demonstrate greater validity than clinical interview methods, there is no clear reason to insist on using a face-to-face interview in this context.

That clinical screening measures have predicted as well as they have to employment and training criteria is perhaps more surprising than if they had not predicted at all. Measures designed for other purposes have limited likelihood of predicting to new criteria unless there is some reason for them to do so. Rather than starting with instruments whose general validity and reliability are well established, but whose applicability to a new task is unknown, a more potentially productive strategy may be to start with problematic on-the-job behaviors and select or design measures with some theoretical relevance to the prediction problem at hand. While measures like the MMPI and the Sixteen Personality Factor Questionnaire (16PF) may be excellent instruments for the clinic, they are not necessarily as appropriate for predicting persons at risk for employment malfeasance on the job. For now, practitioners must proceed with caution in selecting measures to be used for pre-employment screening, and must carefully review validity and reliability evidence specific to the employment setting before deciding on the use of a particular pre-employment screening device.

Issues with Criterion Measures. Overall, the results most supportive of the validity of pre-employment screening measures are those using regression equations to predict membership in "successful" versus "problematic" groups. Though these studies typically result in a high number of false positives and false negatives, they generally predict membership in the defined criterion groups reasonably well. However, this is a rather crude criterion measure, implying simplistic groupings of people into categories. Certainly attrition is a binary criterion (one either is or is not in the workplace on follow-up), but reasons for leaving can be diverse, ranging from deciding a career is not a good fit with an individual, to employee malfeasance or incompetence on the job. The validity of pre-employment screening should be judged primarily against more complex criteria than a simple on/off job criterion. Studies that have looked at more complex outcome criteria have generally been somewhat less supportive of the validity of the pre-employment screening measures.

Differentiating between training and on-the-job criteria is also important. Studies finding that psychological screening devices predict to training criteria (e.g., Mills & Bohannon, 1980) are limited in their relevance for determining on-the-job performance. This situation is commonly encountered in other personnel selection problems (Ghiselli, 1973). It parallels issues involved in using intellectual measures, which predict well to school performance, to predict to real-life criteria such as success at work or in home life. The pre-employment screening

44

validation literature using training rather than on-the-job criteria has generally found the best predictors to be intellectual measures (or their surrogates on personality scales). This is not surprising, since training programs may require much more use of intellectual abilities than will often be the case on the job.

At their best, future validity studies will assess predictability to both training *and* job-performance criteria. Each is an appropriate concern of employers. However, if one or the other must be chosen, "real-life" on-the-job criteria (the most neglected in the literature to date) provide the most convincing evidence of the relationship between psychopathology and work.

The Longitudinal Perspective. Psychological health and impairment are not constant conditions. Job applicants, once screened, are neither forever after free of psychological problems or forever after plagued with impairment. As demonstrated by other prediction problems in the employment context (e.g., Ghiselli & Haire, 1960; Helmreich, Sawin, & Carsrud, 1986), the factors that predict to long- and short-term criteria may differ (Aylward, 1985; Pugh, 1985). This implies the need for validation of pre-employment screening devices against longitudinal criteria if long-term prediction is important.

In general, tests that have been validated against training criteria (i.e., successfully completing a training program) say little about the ability of employees to successfully perform on the job. When long-term predictability is the desired goal, validation research should be designed with this goal in mind. Alternatively, particularly if it is demonstrated that certain patterns of psychopathology are associated with impairment in the performance of certain types of work, and if psychological screening methods only are valid for determining presence of pathology at the time of the assessment, periodic screening of individuals in sensitive jobs or occupations might be needed.

OTHER PROFESSIONAL PRACTICE ISSUES

Although the current state of the literature leaves much to be desired, clinicians in practice may be confronted with conducting pre-employment screening in a less than perfect "real world." Therefore, some recommendations for professional practice in this real world are provided in this section.

At the beginning of pre-employment screening, the clinician needs to establish, with the employer's assistance, exactly what traits and characteristics are being assessed and what, if any, relationship these have to demonstrated problematic behavior on the job. Ideally, this process will take place after an intensive job analysis (see Lowman, 1985, pp. 16-17, for an example of appropriate procedure involving careful assessment of the job characteristics). At the least, psychologists need to assure both themselves and the employer-client that appropriate awareness exists of what psychological screening can and cannot do. A written agreement, in which the psychologist articulates the specific screening protocol and the uses for which it is appropriate, is recommended. For example, the psychologist might specify with the employer an agreement similar to the one shown on pages 48 and 49.

INFORMED CONSENT

APA Ethical Principles require that persons being screened by psychological assessment procedures be advised before their participation of what will happen to them, the risks involved, and the consequences of non-participation. Principle 6 (Welfare of the Consumer) of the APA ethics code states: "Psychologists fully inform consumers as to the purpose and nature of an evaluative, treatment, educational, or training procedure, and they freely acknowledge that clients, students, or participants in research have freedom of choice with regard to participation" (APA, 1981, p. 636). While *Standards for Educational and Psychological Testing* considers such consent to be implied in the case of testing for purposes of employment, even in this case these standards require that "test takers should be informed concerning the testing process" (AERA et al., 1985, p. 85). Because the relevance of screening for psychopathology may not be clear to the job candidate, a formal explanation of the purposes of such assessment is necessary if test takers are to make an informed decision about participation.

The right not to participate in psychological procedures becomes somewhat complex when one is being screened for purposes of potential employment. Certainly, individuals who object to psychological screening need to be informed (if this is the case) that they will receive no further consideration for employment if they do not complete the testing or screening procedures. However, even with such a policy in place, it is desirable to ascertain the candidate's reasons for nonparticipation and, if appropriate, to employ alternative mental health screening procedures.

Confronted with a job applicant who refuses to participate in the psychological screening, the psychologist should meet with the individual and determine the specific objection(s) to testing. Possibly the candidate cannot read well or, especially with applicant populations unsophisticated in test taking, may have very naïve ideas about what screening tests can and cannot do. (In rural locations, or among certain religious groups, candidates might feel that psychological tests will "read the mind" or be used in opposition to certain religious teachings.) Other candidates may object because they have heard that there are test items that ask about very personal issues such as sex or religion. The psychologist faced with such job candidates may need to explain how objective psychological tests are constructed, and in some cases might permit the candidate to leave blank any offensive items. In other cases, job candidates may have had psychological problems and may not want this information to be discovered by the employer.

No data were found in the literature addressing the base rate of refusals to complete psychological tests for pre-employment screening. Presumably, this happens infrequently. If so, the psychologist could possibly spend extra time (not inexpensive) with the occasional applicant who declines participation. If the individual objects only to the particular test used, an alternative test might be considered. If, however, the job candidate refuses all psychological tests, and a legitimate reason for such refusal can be ascertained, a clinical interview might suffice. Alternatively, arrangements might be made for such candidates (who are otherwise acceptable) to be placed in a job with lower security classification or risk factors.

For some candidates who refuse to participate in pre-employment screening, the resistance may reflect more serious psychopathology, including excessive suspiciousness and/or paranoid ideation - conditions which are probably best excluded from employment requiring high-security access, police work, and other sensitive jobs.

SAMPLE MEMORANDUM OF UNDER-
STANDING BETWEEN PSYCHOLOGIST
AND ORGANIZATIONAL CLIENT

Date:

Between: [Psychologist]

And: [Organizational Client]

I [the psychologist] agree to conduct psychological assess-ments of candidates for employment for the position of [police officer] for the [Metropolitan County Sheriff's Department]. It is understood that I will be screening candidates referred by the Department for purposes of determining the presence of psychopathology which may be associated with performance problems during the training program or when on the job. Because there are limitations on what currently available psychological methods can provide for accurately screening out persons who will make poor [police officers], it is recommended that the psychological screening be used as only one part of an overall pre-employment review process in eliminating a candidate from further employment consideration. It should be recognized that a certain portion of those who "fail" the psychological screening process would still be able to perform well in training and on the job, and that a certain portion of those who "pass" will subsequently develop psychological problems which may interfere with their performance on the job.

It is therefore recommended that psychological data be used as only one data source for pre-employment screening. Background checks, prior history, [police] vocational interest, and ability measures all will provide additional information which will clarify the psychological recommendation. In cases in which candidates will otherwise be rejected, coordination between the psychologist assessor and those responsible for collecting and/or interpreting other data sources is recommended. This is also true in cases in which psychological assessment information has resulted in no grounds for rejection, but background data or other information suggests reasons for not hiring.

It is understood and agreed that persons not at apparent psychological risk at the time of the assessment may develop future mental health problems which may interfere with their successful performance on the job. While a good pre-employment screening program will lessen the numbers of [police] who are at higher risk of psychological impairment, it will not eliminate such problems from developing subsequently. Therefore, [the psychologist] strongly recommends that the Department maintain a behavioral observation program by which early signs of psycholog-ical impairment may be noted, and a referral and/or a mental health assessment and treatment program be instituted so that any [police officers] experiencing mental dysfunction may be helped before their difficulties begin to interfere with job perform-ance.

The [Department] recognizes that psychological data are sensitive and can be misused by untrained individuals. Therefore, unless otherwise agreed, [the psychologist] will retain on file all original testing materials and written psychological reports. If, in particular cases, more detailed information is needed, it can be supplied to an appropriately qualified professional. The Department agrees to retain all psychological information in an appropriate, confidential file; to exercise due caution in the use of such data; and to dispose of the data and/or reports when they are no longer current (typically after 1 year).

[Psychologist]	[Date]

[Department Official]	[Date]

Employers appear to be within their legal rights to refuse employment to individuals who do not agree to be screened (see, e.g., Flanagan, 1986). Ethically, in such circumstances the psychologist must clearly advise applicants that, should they choose not to participate (assuming an alternative screening device is not plausible, or severe psychopathology is suspected), they will receive no further consideration for the job.

Even though the ethical issues may be debated, it is probably best that all candidates sign a written statement to the effect that they understand the purposes of the testing, the uses to which the test will be put, and the consequences of nonparticipation. A sample consent form used by the Tennessee Valley Authority for applicants in nuclear power facilities is presented on page 50. Ideally (though it may not always be feasible to do so), the consent form should also make clear who has access to test results, how long they will be retained, and what provisions exist for confidentiality and feedback. In conjunction with this, psychologists must clearly establish systems for protecting the confidentiality of the test materials (APA Ethical Principle 5).

FEEDBACK TO JOB APPLICANTS ON THE RESULTS OF TESTING

What is the right of the person being assessed to know the results of the psychological screening procedures?

SAMPLE CONSENT FORM*

INFORMATION FOR INDIVIDUALS TAKING PSYCHOLOGICAL
TESTING AS PART OF THE PSYCHOLOGICAL SCREENING PROGRAM

As part of your medical examination, you have been asked to complete a psychological test, the Minnesota Multiphasic Personality Inventory (MMPI). This test is being administered because you are an applicant for, or an employee in, a position requiring psychological approval.

This test will provide important information that may enable us to grant you psychological approval. While it is not the type of test that you can "fail," further evaluation may be indicated on the basis of your test results.

If no further evaluation is indicated, a statement of psychological approval will be placed in your medical record.

If further evaluation is indicated, you will be scheduled for a personal interview with a psychologist to complete your evaluation. No individual is ever denied approval solely on the basis of test results.

At any time after you have taken this test, you may request an explanation of your results, which are kept in a confidential file by the Psychological Services Section. If you wish to obtain such feedback, ask someone in the health station or medical office to schedule an appointment with a company psychologist to review your test results.

Data or results obtained from [name of company]'s psychological screening program may be used for research or statistical purposes in a grouped format. However, in any research application, an individual's results will under no circumstance be identifiable, nor will his or her identity otherwise be revealed.

Please sign and date this form below. Your signature indicates that you have read this form and understand the purpose for which psychological testing is to be conducted.

Should you have any questions, please ask your test administrator for assistance.

Your Signature

Social Security Number   Today's Date
---

*This form was provided by, and reproduced with permission of, the Tennessee Valley Authority.

APA ethics, Principle 8, require that psychologists "respect the client's right to know the results, the interpretations made, and the bases for their conclusions and recommendations" (APA, 1981, p. 637). It can be debated who is the client in conducting pre-employment screening, but Principle 6, Welfare of the Consumer, requires that the psychologist who is providing services "at the request of a third party" must clarify "the nature of the relationships to all parties concerned" (APA, 1981, p. 636). This includes clarification of who will receive feedback on the results of the testing. Although the *Standards for Educational and Psychological Testing* list only school, clinical, and counseling applications as requiring test users to provide test takers with an appropriate explanation of test results and recommendations made (AERA et al., 1985, p. 85), and do not mention testing for employment purposes, it is debatable whether screening for psychopathology is most properly conceptualized as "employment testing" or "clinical testing." (In fact, it concerns both.) Those individuals assessed for purposes of employability, and particularly those individuals rejected on the basis of the screening methods, thus should be provided feedback when they desire it. At a minimum, applicants who will receive no feedback on the screening should be so informed at the beginning of the testing procedure as part of an "informed consent" process.

What format this feedback should take can be debated. It does not appear ethically mandatory that an individual be given a copy of any written psychological report provided to potential employers (see, e.g., Lowman, 1985, pp. 12-14). However, the assessee should be provided feedback in a form that can readily be understood. In cases of rejected individuals, this should probably be oral feedback in which the individual can be advised of the decisions made and the psychological basis for making them. A personalized feedback session, for those desiring it, provides more opportunity than a written procedure to explain the results of the testing and to help the client understand the concerns raised by the evaluation. On the other hand, some applicants may be intensely angry at the rejection and seek the feedback session only to ventilate anger or, in extreme cases, to direct threats or litigation against the psychologist. When there is a suspected threat to the personal safety of the psychologist, appropriate precautions should be taken to provide the feedback with another therapist present or with security personnel nearby.

Psychologists should also clearly work out with the potential employer methods by which candidates desiring such feedback should receive it, and how the costs associated with such feedback are to be paid. Feedback in terms the assessee can understand (Ethical Principle 8-a) is probably best given in face-to-face sessions, particularly if the individuals most likely to ask for feedback will be those who have been rejected on the basis of psychological findings. Because face-to-face feedback is time-consuming and expensive, it needs to be carefully budgeted in setting up such programs. Too often, psychologists and potential employers do not adequately consider the feedback issue and appear to hope that, by not mentioning its availability, no one will request it. To avoid later conflicts over who shall bear the costs and burden for such feedback, provisions for feedback elaborated in advance are especially important when an outside contractor is used to conduct the psychological screening.

ADVERTISING AND MARKETING OF PSYCHOLOGICAL SCREENING SERVICES

Psychologists are bound to limit their claims about their services to ones which are consistent with evidence and which do not mislead the consumer or exaggerate the likely results of using the services. As the APA ethical principles state:

> *Principle 4-b (Public Statements).* [Public statements] do not contain (i) a false, fraudulent, misleading, deceptive, or unfair statement; (ii) a misrepresentation of fact or a statement likely to mislead or deceive because in context it makes only a partial disclosure of relevant facts; . . . (iv) a statement intended or likely to create false or unjustified expectations of favorable results. (APA, 1981, p. 635).

Considering the state of present knowledge outlined in this book, it would be easy to overpromise what psychological screening programs can and cannot do. For example, one popularly used computerized interpretation program claims that its report helps to "identify individuals emotionally unsuitable for high-stress, high-risk work." The advertisement also states that its method of interpreting the MMPI will "evaluate personality attributes that might contribute to unsafe, irresponsible or ineffective on-the-job behavior in the specific positions listed below . . . The evaluations . . . take into account . . . the job for which the applicant is applying."

Does this mean that the authors have done a job analysis of the specific positions for which evaluation is sought? Has the vendor validated the MMPI against job criteria in the particular applicant population? If such validation efforts have occurred, they have not appeared in the published literature. What seems more likely is that the authors of this procedure have a data base which includes applicants from specified positions, and that they are making recommendations relative to that normative group. If "taking into account" merely refers to a set of occupational-specific test norms, this type of methodology should be differentiated from one that has actually validated specific test patterns for particular occupational groups against job-related criteria.

The use of computerized testing itself suggests important ethical issues. A review of these complex issues is beyond the scope of this guide (see, however, Eyde & Kowal, 1987). However, claims like the ones cited here may mislead users of such services if they imply that there is a preponderance of validity evidence against job-related criteria for specific psychological tests. Regrettably, claims by those marketing pre-employment screening may have misled consumers by suggesting greater validity than presently exists.

Purveyors of test-interpretation services and psychologists who conduct pre-employment mental health screening need to reconcile their advertising and public announcements with the limits of knowledge in this field. If, as has been argued here, the validity evidence for psychological screening is severely limited at this time, psychologists must circumspectly describe what their services can and cannot be expected to do. They should give special attention to acknowledging and communicating limitations. In helping employers set up a psychological screening program, psychologists should work to obtain a comprehensive and legally defensible overall screening program. They should avoid misleading employers into thinking their methods are foolproof or that additional information (e.g., that provided by background checks) is not necessary.

SUMMARY OF PROFESSIONAL
PRACTICE RECOMMENDATIONS

This section will summarize the major points developed in more detail in the guide. For those inclined to begin with or to read only this section, a number of important points are discussed in the text concerning specific methodologies recommended for use. Because of the complexities and unresolved issues in this field, pre-employment screening is not an area to rush into quickly from a "once over lightly" reading to practice. The unresolved questions of validity are sufficiently complex that practitioners can create many problems for themselves by proceeding in a superficial or undisciplined manner.

REACH CONSENSUS ON SCREENING CRITERIA

Before determining that it is appropriate to conduct pre-employment screening, the practitioner should carefully review the work, if any, that has been done to determine the characteristics or behavior of persons who are held to be problematic on the job. Consensual validation is better than nothing, but it alone is not enough. Hakel and Schuh (1971) long ago demonstrated that consensus about "desirable" applicant qualities can be reached rather easily and appears to cut across diverse occupations. Unfortunately, however, the consensus on "screen-in" desired characteristics often reads like a Boy Scout list of virtues, and the specific job relevancy has yet to be demonstrated. Consensus on "screen-out" criteria recommended by experts may similarly be overly general or idealized. The consensus, even of so-called experts, can be wrong. For example, a group of job experts might concur that sociopathy is a contraindication for hiring for a position in the police or federal government. Yet, at least preliminary evidence suggests that some of the best police officers may have subclinical elevations on the "4-9" scales of the MMPI. Accordingly, job experts should agree on the characteristics to be screened out; ideally, there should also be validity evidence available to support the job-relatedness of the characteristics being screened out.

The costs of conducting this job-related review should not be underestimated. It is time-consuming and expensive to determine valid contraindications to employment in a particular occupation or position. Above all, the mental health professional should not assume that psychopathology *per se* is counterproductive to working in a particular job or line of work. At best, psychologists can describe behavior that is now problematic (but that may not be with treatment) or patterns of behavior that may be associated with a higher risk of eventual on-the-job problems. At worst, clinicians will make a number of unfounded statements about a person's employability which may later be the subject of litigation should someone inappropriately be turned down for a position.

Although, in the case of police and nuclear power industry personnel, research has been sponsored on the use of psychological methods for personnel screening (e.g., Buchanan, Davis, & Dunnette, 1981; U.S. Nuclear Regulatory Commission, Office of Nuclear Regulatory Research, 1981), no consensus yet exists on what criteria should be screened out and by what methods. This conclusion applies even more to other occupational groups for which little effort has been made to define "screen-out" criteria. Research attention needs to be directed to reaching greater consensus on undesirable characteristics to be screened out, and to making a careful determination of the validity evidence for the specific criteria to be screened out. If certain criteria are not being measured by existing screening methods but are important in predicting dysfunctions on the job, new tests may need to be developed and validated for these purposes. If, however, an employer or occupational group can be satisfied with those characteristics of behavior or of individuals in the present, the psychological screening task can be executed with more consistency. As long as agreement is absent on the behaviors or characteristics that are undesirable and to be weeded out, there cannot be consistency from one screening process to another in evaluating applicants. In such a case, the practitioner risks practicing (or being charged with practicing) inappropriately.

CLEARLY IDENTIFY SCREENING
CRITERIA AND SPECIFY RESERVATIONS

While there can be disagreement on the nature of the pre-employment screening task, the psychologist should clearly indicate the criteria actually employed in a particular screening assignment. If no situationally specific criteria were used (relying instead on generic characteristics of persons thought to be counterindicators to employability, such as the approach used by Butcher's [1983] computerized MMPI interpretation), this should clearly be stated to avoid overgeneralizing or misunderstanding by the user. Where appropriate, a carefully worded statement explaining the limitations of the assessment methodology can be included with each assessment. This may also help the clinician defend any screening method that may subsequently be litigated.

A number of reservations generally need to be voiced in any screening that results in rejection of a candidate on the basis of psychological problems. First, the rejection may be based on behavior that is subject to change over time. This is particularly true for young people being assessed, since their patterns of deviation may be subject to change or self-correction with age. Applicants rejected on the basis of psychological problems should be advised (if true) of the possibility of reapplying at a later time. Second, persons determined to be psychologically fit for duty may prove at a later time to be unfit for duty. The psychologist should never imply, directly or indirectly, that pre-employment screening is valid for the duration of employment of the individual, or that persons with minimal problems will not need mental health treatment intervention over the course of their lifetimes.

ENCOURAGE AND CONDUCT VALIDITY RESEARCH

The validity of psychological screening for purposes of employment appears, on close examination, to be far from proven. While certain types of psychopathology can accurately be identified and screened out in applicant pools, a clear and consistent relationship has not yet been demonstrated between scoring in a psychopathological direction on various screening measures and having performance problems on the job. There is some, but not decisive, evidence that individuals scoring above designated criterion levels on selection devices will, on average, experience more problems on the job than those scoring below those levels. However, there appear to be an unacceptably large number of individuals who would be "false positives" when their psychopathology is compared to job-related criteria. This is especially true, current literature suggests, for individuals with personality disorders. Much more research is needed to determine what characteristics of psychopathology are associated with poor job performance and to determine the intervening variables that enable some individuals with displayed psychopathology to perform satisfactorily on the job.

Moreover, the studies that have been reported in the professional literature to date have used limited criterion measures and have not followed individuals over time to determine the lasting validity of pre-employment screening.

OBTAIN "INFORMED CONSENT" FROM JOB APPLICANTS

While some argue that there is implied consent whenever applicants are assessed prior to employment, in the case of mental health screening, there is sufficient controversy and potential misunderstanding that psychologists should get consent regardless of what they think may be legally necessary. A simple statement that the assessee understands the purpose of the screening, what will happen to the data collected, the procedures (if any) for obtaining feedback on the results of evaluation, and what appeal procedure(s), if any, are available for the weeded-out applicant should suffice. If there are restrictions on ability to obtain feedback or appeal, these should be communicated at the time the person applies for the job. The documentation of informed consent can be assured by requiring applicants to sign a written statement to the effect that the purposes of the testing have been explained to them, they consent to the testing procedure, and they understand what will happen to the data they provide.

Individuals objecting to psychological testing should, if possible, be given an alternative means for proving psychological fitness, assuming there is a legitimate cause for the objections and assuming that an alternative evaluation procedure with similar validity is available. Some individuals may simply need more information. Candidates, for example, who object to religious and sexual items on the MMPI might need a thorough explanation of why these items are included and how they relate to the overall testing procedures. Individuals finding the evaluation procedures objectionable (e.g., an invasion of privacy) should be given the opportunity to state their position, and a reasonable attempt should be made to find a satisfactory resolution of the objections.

PROTECT THE RIGHTS OF THOSE
REJECTED BY PSYCHOLOGICAL SCREENING

Those individuals rejected on the basis of psychological screening tests need to be provided (when they request it) with explanations of the basis of their rejection. Applicants should have an appeal procedure available if they desire to contest the decisions made about them. In the case of rejection for mental health reasons, a reasonable appeals process might allow the unsuccessful candidate to be assessed by a psychologist or psychiatrist of the person's choice, and both reports submitted to a third mental health professional. Since psychopathology is often fluctuating or variable in its course over time, there should also be an opportunity for applicants rejected for mental health reasons to reapply after a reasonable period of time - say, 1 year - especially if the reasons for their rejection are unlikely to be long-lasting (e.g., a reactive depression after the death of a parent).

PROVIDE FEEDBACK WHEN IT IS REQUESTED

Applicants who undergo psychological testing as part of a job application process should be provided feedback when they request it. Not all individuals want it, even among those who are rejected. However, employers and psychologist(s) are advised to have a policy in place to notify the applicants of the procedures they may use to obtain feedback on the results of testing. Ideally, this feedback, at least in cases of rejection, would be given face-to-face by a qualified psychologist or other mental health professional. Funds for this purpose need to be budgeted as part of the initial screening process. If there is to be no access to test results and no feedback process, this too should be clearly communicated at the time of obtaining informed consent. The effects of such a policy on the validity of the test results are unknown.

PROTECT THE CONFIDENTIALITY
OF PSYCHOLOGICAL DATA

Raw psychological data and psychological test reports need to be maintained in a secure, limited-access archival system. Generally, psychologists or other mental health professionals should be the custodians of psychological data. Release of data should be guided by strict, carefully considered policies; exceptions to confidentiality should be made extremely sparingly and with clear and compelling cause. If reports are to be provided to employers, they should be in language the employer can understand. This also applies to any written reports that are prepared for applicants who have been screened.

RECOGNIZE THAT PSYCHOLOGICAL SCREENING ALONE IS INSUFFICIENT

Even carefully screened groups of employees are not immune to the subsequent development of job-related psychopathology. Organizations with ongoing security needs are advised to monitor behavior on the job after hiring. Some employers (e.g., Beutler et al., 1985) recommend routinely screening such groups as police every few years. In addition, employers are well advised to install employee assistance programs (Lowman, in press) staffed by highly qualified mental health professionals, to assure that those employees who develop mental problems after hiring will be able to receive help with the approval of management at an early rather than later stage of dysfunction.

REFERENCES

Aita, J. A. (1949). Efficacy of the brief clinical interview method in predicting adjustments. *Archives of Neurology and Psychiatry, 61,* 170-176.

American Educational Research Association, American Psychological Association, and National Council on Measurement in Education. (1985). *Standards for Educational and Psychological Testing.* Washington, DC: American Psychological Association.

American Nuclear Society. (1982). *American National Standard. Security for Nuclear Power Plants* (ANSI/ANS-3.3-1982). La Grange Park, IL: American Nuclear Society.

American Psychological Association. (1981). Ethical principles of psychologists. *American Psychologist, 36,* 633-638.

American Psychological Association, Committee on Professional Standards. (1982). Casebook for providers of psychological services. *American Psychologist, 37,* 698-701.

American Psychological Association, Committee on Professional Standards. (1983). Casebook for providers of psychological services. *American Psychologist, 38,* 708-713.

American Psychological Association, Committee on Professional Standards. (1984). Casebook for providers of psychological services. *American Psychologist, 39,* 663-668.

American Psychological Association. (1987). *Casebook on Ethical Principles of Psychologists.* Washington, DC: Author.

Anastasi, A. (1984, November 26). Letter to U.S. Nuclear Regulatory Commission.

Arvey, R. D., Mussio, S. J., & Payne, G. (1972). Relationships between MMPI scores and job performance measures of firefighters. *Psychological Reports, 31,* 199-202.

Aylward, J. (1985). Psychological testing and police selection. *Journal of Police Science and Administration, 13,* 201-210.

Azen, S. P., Snibbe, H. M., & Montgomery, H. P. (1973). A longitudinal predictive study of success and performance of law enforcement officers. *Journal of Applied Psychology, 57,* 190-192.

Bartol, C. R. (1982). Psychological characteristics of small-town police officers. *Journal of Police Science and Administration, 10,* 58-63.

Bellack, A. S., & Morrison, R. L. (1982). Interpersonal dysfunction. In A. S. Bellack, M. Hersen, & A. E. Kazan (Eds.), *International Handbook of Behavior Modification and Theory* (pp. 717-747). New York: Plenum Press.

Berghausen, P. E., Jr. (1985). Access authorization: Interview everyone--Psychometrics alone is unethical and unsafe. *Transactions of the American Nuclear Society, 50,* 644.

Beutler, L. E., Storm, A., Kirkish, P., Scogin, F., & Gaines, J. A. (1985). Parameters in the prediction of police officer performance. *Professional Psychology, 16,* 324-335.

Borofsky, G. L. (1987). *Screening for Unreliable Behavior in the Nuclear Industry.* Paper presented at the annual meeting of American Nuclear Society, Dallas, TX.

Brill, N. W., & Beebe, G. W. (1952). Some applications of a follow-up study to psychiatric standards for mobilization. *American Journal of Psychiatry, 109,* 401-410.

Buchanan, J. C., Davis, S. O., & Dunnette, M. D. (1981). *Behavioral Reliability Program for the Nuclear Industry* (NUREG/CR-2076). Washington, DC: U.S. Nuclear Regulatory Commission.

Burbeck, E., & Furnham, A. (1985). Police officer selection: A critical review of the literature. *Journal of Police Science and Administration, 13,* 58-69.

Butcher, J. N. (1979). Use of the MMPI in personnel selection. In J. N. Butcher (Ed.), *New Developments in the Use of the MMPI* (pp. 165-201). Minneapolis: University of Minnesota Press.

Butcher, J. N. (1983). *The Minnesota Personnel Interpretive Report*. Minneapolis: University of Minnesota.

Butcher, J. N. (1985). Personality assessment in industry: Theoretical issues and illustrations. In H. J. Bernardin & D. A. Bownas (Eds.), *Personality Assessment in Organizations* (pp. 277-309). New York: Praeger.

Callan, J. P. (1972). An attempt to use the MMPI as a predictor of failure in military training. *British Journal of Psychiatry, 121,* 553-557.

Carlson, H., Thayer, R. E., & Germann, A. C. (1971). Social attitudes and personality differences among members of two kinds of police departments (innovative vs. traditional) and students. *Journal of Criminal Law, Criminology & Political Science, 62,* 564-567.

Carpenter, B. N., & Raza, S. M. (1987). Personality characteristics of police applicants: Comparisons across subgroups and with other populations. *Journal of Police Science and Administration, 15,* 10-17.

Caveny, E. L. (1955). The utilization of psychiatric marginal manpower in military service. *Annals of Internal Medicine, 42,* 659-667.

Christy, R. L., & Rasmussen, J. E. (1963). Human reliability implications of the U.S. Navy's experience in screening and selection procedure. *American Journal of Psychiatry, 120,* 540-547.

Colligan, M. J., Smith, M. J., & Hurrell, J. J. (1977). Occupational incidence rates of mental health disorders. *Journal of Human Stress, 32,* 34-39.

Costello, R. M., Schoenfeld, L. S., & Kobos, J. (1982). Police applicant screening: An analogue study. *Journal of Clinical Psychology, 38,* 216-221.

Curran, J. P., & Monti, P. M. (Eds.). (1982). *Social Skills Training*. New York: Guilford Press.

Daniels, E. E., & Hunter, W. A. (1949). MMPI personality patterns for various occupations. *Journal of Applied Psychology, 33,* 559-565.

Egan, J. R., Jackson, L., & Eames, R. H. (1951). A study of neuropsychiatric rejectees. *Journal of the American Association, 145,* 466-469.

Evans, D. R. (1976). The use of the MMPI to predict conscientious hotline workers. *Journal of Clinical Psychology, 32,* 684-686.

Eyde, L. D. (1987). Computerised psychological testing: An introduction. *Applied Psychology: An International Review, 36,* 223-235.

Eyde, L. D., & Kowal, D. M. (1987). Computerised test interpretation services: Ethical and professional concerns regarding U.S. producers and users. *Applied Psychology: An International Review, 36,* 401-417.

Flanagan, C. L. (1986, August). *Legal Considerations in Psychological Screening for High Risk Occupations.* Paper presented at the annual meeting of the American Psychological Association, Washington, DC.

Ghiselli, E. E. (1973). The validity of aptitude tests in personnel selection. *Personnel Psychology, 26,* 461-477.

Ghiselli, E. E., & Haire, M. (1960). The validation of selection tests in the light of dynamic character of criteria. *Personnel Psychology, 13,* 225-231.

Glass, A. J., Ryan, F. J., Lubin, A., Ramana, C. V., & Tucker, A. C. (1956). Psychiatric prediction and military effectiveness. *U.S. Armed Forces Medical Journal, 7,* 1427-1443.

Greene, R. L. (1980). *The MMPI: An Interpretative Manual.* New York: Grune & Stratton.

Gruber, G. (1986). The Police Applicant Test: A predictive validity study. *Journal of Police Science and Administration, 14,* 121-129.

Guion, R. M., & Gottier, R. F. (1965). Validity of personality measures in personnel selection. *Personnel Psychology, 18,* 135-164.

Gynther, M. D., Altman, H., & Warbin, R. W. (1973). Behavioral correlates for the Minnesota Multiphasic Personality Inventory 4-9, 9-4 code types: A case of the emperor's new clothes? *Journal of Consulting and Clinical Psychology, 40,* 259-263.

Hakel, M. D., & Schuh, A. J. (1971). Job applicant attributes judged important across seven diverse occupations. *Personnel Psychology, 24,* 45-52.

Hargrave, G. E. (1985). Using the MMPI and CPI to screen law enforcement applicants: A study of reliability and validity of clinicians' decisions. *Journal of Police Science and Administration, 13,* 221-224.

Hargrave, G. E., & Berner, J. G. (1984). *POST Psychological Screening Manual.* Sacramento: California Commission on Peace Officer Standards and Training.

Hargrave, G. E., & Hiatt, D. (1987). Law enforcement selection with the interview, MMPI, and CPI: A study of reliability and validity. *Journal of Police Science and Administration, 15,* 110-117.

Hargrave, G. E., Hiatt, D., & Gaffney, T. W. (1986). A comparison of MMPI and CPI test profiles for traffic officers and deputy sheriffs. *Journal of Police Science and Administration, 14,* 250-258.

Harrell, T. W. (1972). High earning MBA's. *Personnel Psychology, 25,* 523-530.

Harrell, T. W., & Harrell, M. S. (1972). The personality of MBA's who reach general management early. *Personnel Psychology, 26,* 127-134.

Hedlund, D. E. (1965). A review of the MMPI in industry. *Psychological Reports, 17,* 875-889.

Helmreich, R. L., Sawin, L. L., & Carsrud, A. L. (1986). The honeymoon effect in job performance: Temporal increases in the predictive power of achievement motivation. *Journal of Applied Psychology, 71,* 185-188.

Hogan, R. (1971). Personality characteristics of highly rated policemen. *Personnel Psychology, 24,* 679-686.

Hogan, R., Carpenter, B. N., Briggs, S. R., & Hansson, R. O. (1985). Personality assessment and personnel selection. In H. J. Bernardin & D. A. Bownas (Eds.), *Personality Assessment in Organizations* (pp. 21-52). New York: Praeger.

Hogan, R., & Kurtines, W. (1975). Personological correlates of police effectiveness. *Journal of Psychology, 91,* 289-295.

Holland, J. L. (1985). *Making Vocational Choices* (2nd ed.). Englewood Cliffs, NJ: Prentice-Hall.

Hunt, W. A., Wittson, C. L., & Burton, H. W. (1950a). A further validation of naval neuropsychiatric screening. *Journal of Consulting Psychology, 14,* 485-488.

Hunt, W. A., Wittson, C. L., & Burton, H. W. (1950b). A validation study of naval neuropsychiatric screening. *Journal of Consulting Psychology, 14,* 35-39.

Hunt, W. A., Wittson, C. L., & Hunt, E. G. (1952a). Military performance of a group of marginal neuropsychiatric cases. *American Journal of Psychiatry, 109,* 168-171.

Hunt, W. A., Wittson, C. L., & Hunt, E. G. (1952b). Relationship between definiteness of psychiatric diagnosis and severity of disability. *Journal of Clinical Psychology, 8,* 314-315.

Hunt, W. A., Wittson, C. L., & Hunt, E. G. (1954). Hidden costs in the utilization of the psychiatrically marginal man. *Journal of Clinical Psychology, 10,* 91-92.

Inwald, R. E. (1985). Proposed guidelines for conducting pre-employment psychological screening programs. *Crime Control Digest, 19*(11), 1-6.

Inwald, R. E., Knatz, H., & Shusman, E. (1982). *The Inwald Personality Inventory Manual.* Kew Gardens, NY: Hilson.

Inwald, R. E., & Shusman, E. J. (1984a). Personality and performance sex differences of law enforcement officer recruits. *Journal of Police Science and Administration, 12,* 339-347.

Inwald, R. E., & Shusman, E. J. (1984b). The IPI and MMPI as predictors of academy performance of police recruits. *Police Science and Administration, 12*(3), 1-11.

Jamison, K. (1985). *Manic Depressive Illness.* New York: Oxford University Press.

Lavin, P. F., Chardos, S. P., Ford, T. W, & McGee, R. K. (1987, June). *MMPI Profiles of Troubled Employees in Relation to Nuclear Power Plant Personnel Norms.* Paper presented at the annual meeting of the American Nuclear Society, Dallas, TX.

London, M., & Bray, D. W. (1980). Ethical issues in testing and evaluation for personnel decisions. *American Psychologist, 35,* 890-901.

Lowman, R. L. (Ed.). (1985). *Casebook on Ethics and Standards for the Practice of Psychology in Organizations.* College Park, MD: Society for Industrial and Organizational Psychology, Inc., Division 14 of the American Psychological Association.

Lowman, R. L. (in press). Managing external employee assistance programs. In J. W. Jones, B. D. Steffy, & D. W. Bray (Eds.), *Applying Psychology in Business: The Manager's Handbook.* Lexington, MA: Lexington Books.

Lowman, R. L., & Leeman, G. E. (1988). The dimensionality of social intelligence: Abilities, interests and personality. *Journal of Psychology, 122,* 279-290.

Lowman, R. L., & Parker, D. F. (1988). *Symptoms of Work-Related Anxiety and Depression in a Longitudinal, Employed, Cross-Organizational Longitudinal Sample.* Manuscript in review.

Masahiko, T., et al. (1983). A study of the response of the medical school students to the MMPI during and after the entrance examination. *Journal of Behaviormetrics [Japanese], 10,* 28-39. [English translation from *Psychological Abstracts,* 1984, *71,* Abstract No. 29757.]

Matarazzo, J. D., Allen, B. V., Saslaw, G., & Wiens, A. N. (1964). Characteristics of successful policemen and firemen applicants. *Journal of Applied Psychology, 48,* 123-133.

Megargee, E. I. (1972). *The California Psychological Inventory Handbook.* San Francisco: Jossey-Bass.

Meier, R. D., Farmer, R. E., & Maxwell, D. (1987). Psychological screening of police candidates: Current perspectives. *Journal of Police Science and Administration, 15,* 210-215.

Mills, C. J., & Bohannon, W. E. (1980). Personality characteristics of effective state police officers. *Journal of Applied Psychology, 65,* 680-684.

Mirvis, P. H., & Seashore, S. E. (1979). Being ethical in organizational research. *American Psychologist, 34,* 766-780.

Muha, T. M., & May, J. R. (1973). An employment index for identifying unfit job applicants. *Journal of Community Psychology, 1,* 362-365.

National Advisory Commission on Criminal Justice Standards and Goals: Police. (1967). Washington, DC: U.S. Government Printing Office.

National Institute of Mental Health. (1985). *Mental Health, United States, 1985* (DHHS Publication No. ADM 85-1378). Washington, DC: Superintendent of Documents, U.S. Government Printing Office.

Parisher, D., Rios, B., & Reilley, R. R. (1979). Psychologists and psychological services in urban police departments: A national survey. *Professional Psychology, 10,* 6-7.

Pugh, G. (1985). The California Psychological Inventory and police selection. *Journal of Police Science and Administration, 13,* 172-177.

Raines, G. N., Wittson, C. L., Hunt, W. A., & Herrmann, R. S. (1954). Psychiatric selection for military service. *Journal of the American Medical Association, 156,* 817-821.

Rhead, C., Abrams, A., Grossman, H., & Margolis, P. (1968). The psychological assessment of police candidates. *American Journal of Psychiatry, 124,* 1575-1580.

Sacuzzo, D. P., Higgins, G., & Lewandowski, D. (1974). Program for psychological assessment of law enforcement officers: Initial evaluation. *Psychological Reports, 35,* 651-654.

Sajwaj, T., Ford, T. W., & McGee, R. K. (1987, June). *Psychological Characteristics of Licensed Nuclear Power Plant Operators.* Paper presented at the annual meeting of the American Nuclear Society, Dallas, TX.

Saxe, S. J., & Reiser, M. (1976). A comparison of three police applicant groups using the MMPI. *Journal of Police Science and Administration, 4,* 419-425.

Schmidt, F. L., Hunter, J. E., Pearlman, K., & Hirsh, H. R. (1985). Forty questions about validity generalization and meta-analysis. *Personnel Psychology, 38,* 697-798.

Schmitt, N. (1976). Social and situational determinants of interview decisions: Implications for the employment interview. *Personnel Psychology, 29,* 79-101.

Schoenfeld, L. S., Kobos, J. C., & Phinney, I. R. (1980). Screening police applicants: A study of reliability with the MMPI. *Psychological Reports, 47,* 419-425.

Scogin, F., & Beutler, L. E. (1986). Psychological screening of law enforcement candidates. In P. A. Keller & L. G. Ritt (Eds.), *Innovations in Clinical Practice: A Source Book* (Vol. 5, pp. 317-330). Sarasota, FL: Professional Resource Exchange, Inc.

Shusman, E. J., Inwald, R. E., & Knatz, H. F. (1987). A cross-validation study of police recruit performance as predicted by the IPI and MMPI. *Journal of Police Science and Administration, 15,* 162-169.

Shusman, E. J., Inwald, R. E., & Landa, B. (1984). Correction officer job performance as predicted by the IPI and MMPI: A validation and cross-validation study. *Criminal Justice and Behavior, 11,* 309-329.

Sutker, P. B., & Allain, A. N. (1983). Behavior and personality assessment in men labelled adaptive sociopaths. *Journal of Behavioral Assessment, 5,* 65-79.

U.S. Nuclear Regulatory Commission. (1984). *Federal Register, 49* (No. 149), 30726-30734.

U.S. Nuclear Regulatory Commission. (1988, March 9). *Federal Register, 53* (No. 46), 7534-7539.

U.S. Nuclear Regulatory Commission, Office of Nuclear Regulatory Research. (1981). *Standards for Psychological Assessment of Nuclear Facility Personnel* (NUREG/-CR-2075 1S). Washington, DC: Author.

U.S. Nuclear Regulatory Commission, Office of Nuclear Regulatory Research. (1984). *Standard Format and Content Guide for Access Authorization Plans for Nuclear Power Plants.* Washington, DC: Author.

Verniaud, W. M. (1946). Occupational differences in the Minnesota Multiphasic Personality Inventory. *Journal of Applied Psychology, 30,* 604-613.

Whyte, W. H., Jr. (1956). *The Organization Man.* New York: Simon & Schuster.

Wiens, A. N., & Matarazzo, J. D. (1983). Diagnostic interviewing. In M. Hersen, A. E. Kazdin, & A. S. Bellack (Eds.), *The Clinical Psychology Handbook* (pp. 309-328). New York: Pergamon Press.

Wittson, C. L., Hunt, W. A., & Stevenson, I. (1946). A follow-up study of neuropsychiatric screening. *Journal of Abnormal and Social Psychology, 41,* 79-82.

OTHER TITLES IN THE PRACTITIONER'S RESOURCE SERIES

Pre-Employment Screening for Psychopathology: A Guide to Professional Practice is one of 10 books now available in the Practitioner's Resource Series. The other published titles are:

Assessment and Treatment of Multiple Personality and Dissociative Disorders by James P. Bloch.
Code ATMH   ISBN #0-943158-67-2   1991   Approx. 92 pp.

Clinical Guidelines for Involuntary Outpatient Treatment by J. Reid Meloy, Ansar Haroun, and Eugene F. Schiller.
Code IOTH   ISBN #0-943158-45-1   1990   78pp.

Cognitive Therapy for Personality Disorders: A Schema-Focused Approach by Jeffrey E. Young.
Code CTPDH   ISBN #0-943158-46-X   1990   90pp.

Dealing with Anger Problems: Rational-Emotive Therapeutic Interventions by Windy Dryden.
Code DAPH   ISBN #0-943158-59-1   1990   62pp.

Diagnosis and Treatment Selection for Anxiety Disorders by Samuel Knapp and Leon VandeCreek.
Code DTSH   ISBN #0-943158-30-3   1989   94pp.

Neuropsychological Evaluation of Head Injury by Lawrence C. Hartlage.
Code NEHIH   ISBN #0-943158-47-8   1990   68pp.

Outpatient Treatment of Child Molesters by Stan Friedman.
Code OTCMH   ISBN #0-943158-65-6   1991   64pp.

Tarasoff *and Beyond: Legal and Clinical Considerations in the Treatment of Life-Endangering Patients* by Leon VandeCreek and Samuel Knapp.

Code TABH   ISBN #0-943158-31-1   1989   74pp.

What Every Therapist Should Know About AIDS by Samuel Knapp and Leon VandeCreek.

Code AIDSH   ISBN #0-943158-58-3   1990   80pp.

Cost per paperback book: $11.70 (includes shipping)
Foreign orders add an additional $1.25 per book

All orders from individuals and private institutions must be prepaid in full. Florida residents add 7%. Prices and availability subject to change without notice.

TO ORDER

To order by mail, please send name, address, and telephone number, along with check or credit card information (card number and expiration date) to:

Professional Resource Exchange, Inc.
PO Box 15560
Sarasota, FL 34277-1560

For fastest service
(VISA/MasterCard/American Express orders only)
CALL 1-813-366-7913
or
FAX 1-813-366-7971

If you'd like to receive a copy of our latest newsletter/catalog, please write or call. Include your professional affiliation (e.g., psychologist, clinical social worker, marriage and family therapist, mental health counselor, school psychologist, psychiatrist, etc.) to be assured of receiving all appropriate mailings.

Thank You!

Some of the Other Titles Available from Professional Resource Exchange, Inc.

Innovations in Clinical Practice: A Source Book - **10 Volumes**
    Hardbound edition (Vols. 3-10 only) per volume.. $54.20
    Looseleaf binder edition (Vols. 1-10) per volume... $59.20
Cognitive Therapy with Couples.. $17.70
Maximizing Third-Party Reimbursement in Your Mental Health Practice................. $32.70
Who Speaks for the Children?
    The Handbook of Individual and Class Child Advocacy... $43.70
Post-Traumatic Stress Disorder:
    Assessment, Differential Diagnosis, and Forensic Evaluation............................. $27.70
Clinical Evaluations of School-Aged Children: A Structured Approach to
    the Diagnosis of Child and Adolescent Mental Disorders................................... $22.70
Stress Management Training: A Group Leader's Guide... $14.70
Stress Management Workbook for Law Enforcement Officers.................................. $ 8.70
Fifty Ways to Avoid Malpractice:
    A Guidebook for Mental Health Professionals.. $17.70
Keeping Up the Good Work:
    A Practitioner's Guide to Mental Health Ethics.. $16.70
Think Straight! Feel Great! 21 Guides to Emotional Self-Control............................. $14.70
Computer-Assisted Psychological Evaluations:
    How to Create Testing Programs in BASIC... $22.70

All prices include shipping charges. Foreign orders add an additional $1.25 per book. All orders from individuals and private institutions must be prepaid in full. Florida residents add 7%. Prices and availability subject to change without notice.

TO ORDER

To order by mail, please send name, address, and telephone number, along with check or credit card information (card number and expiration date) to:

Professional Resource Exchange, Inc.
PO Box 15560
Sarasota, FL 34277-1560

For fastest service
(VISA/MasterCard/American Express orders only)
CALL 1-813-366-7913
or
FAX 1-813-366-7971

If you'd like to receive a copy of our latest newsletter/catalog, please write or call. Include your professional affiliation (e.g., psychologist, clinical social worker, marriage and family therapist, mental health counselor, school psychologist, psychiatrist, etc.) to be assured of receiving all appropriate mailings.

Would You Like To Be On Our Mailing List?

If so, please write, call, or fax the following information:

Name:_____

Address:_____

Address:_____

City/State/Zip:_____

To insure that we send you all appropriate mailings, please include your professional affiliation (e.g., psychologist, clinical social worker, marriage and family therapist, mental health counselor, school psychologist, psychiatrist, etc.).

Professional Resource Exchange, Inc.
PO Box 15560
Sarasota, FL 34277-1560

CALL 1-813-366-7913
or
FAX 1-813-366-7971